A MODERN DE QUINCEY

ASIAN  VISAGES

PORTRAITS   D'ASIE

A MODERN DE QUINCEY

Autobiography of an Opium Addict

H. R. Robinson

with a Foreword and Introduction by
Gerry Abbott

Orchid Press

Herbert R. Robinson (1896-1965)
A MODERN DE QUINCEY: Autobiography of an Opium Addict

First English edition 1942
Second edition 2004

ORCHID PRESS
P.O. Box 19,
Yuttitham Post Office,
Bangkok, 10907 Thailand
www.orchidbooks.com

Copyright © Orchid Press 2004, 2020 by copyright under the terms of the International Copyright Union: all rights reserved. No part of this publication may be reproduced in any form or by any means, electronic or mechanical, including photocopying, recording, or by any information storage or retrieval system without prior permission in writing from the publisher.

Cover illustration: Kachin tribeswoman standing in a poppy field; Kachin State, Burma, circa 1930. Photograph by James H. Green. Courtesy the James Henry Green Collection, Royal Pavilion, Libraries and Museums, Brighton & Hove, UK.

ISBN 978-974-524-038-4

Contents

List of illustrations	vi
Foreword to the second edition by Gerry Abbott	vii
Introduction to the second edition by Gerry Abbott	ix
References	xv
Appendix—book review by George Orwell	xvi
Map of Burma	xviii
Preface	xix
Foreword—Visions of the Past (1896-1914)	xx
Chapter I. The Road to Mandalay	1
Chapter II. A Burmese Interlude	6
Chapter III. The North-east Frontier	10
Chapter IV. A Himalayan Love Interlude	16
Chapter V. On Tour	22
Chapter VI. Devil's Dice	28
Chapter VII. A Touch of Magic	31
Chapter VIII. The Five Virgins	35
Chapter IX. 'Come You Back to Mandalay'	40
Chapter X. The Inner Room	42
Chapter XI. Opium	45
Chapter XII. The Dream	48
Chapter XIII. The Warning	52
Chapter XIV. The Yellow Robe (I)	56
Chapter XV. The Yellow Robe (II)	59
Chapter XVI. The Yellow Robe (III)	63
Chapter XVII. Slaves of the Lamp	71
Chapter XVIII. Plague in Mandalay	74
Chapter XIX. The Purveyor of Charms	78
Chapter XX. The House of the Deer	80

Chapter XXI. A Night in the Jungle and a Decision   87
Chapter XXII. The Last Chance   91
Chapter XXIII. The Return   95
Chapter XXIV. The Abyss   99
Chapter XXV. The Beginning of the End   105
Chapter XXVI. 'It is Finished'   110
Chapter XXVII. Burma Road   115

Illustrations

1. Captain Robinson in 1919   9
2. Captain Robinson in 1923   27
3. Robinson as a Buddhist monk   67
4. Little Ba Set, The Ever-Faithful 101
5. The author today [1942]   117

Foreword to the second edition

It was a small item in *The Guardian* (London) that drew my attention to Captain Robinson's autobiography. What stimulated my curiosity was not so much that the book was largely set in Burma, a special subject of mine, as that the volume was said to be 'unaccountably rare (it hardly ever turns up secondhand)'. Being a book-lover, I tried to acquire a copy of my own through book fairs, the Internet, book-search agents and second-hand bookshops. None could produce a copy. Through the good offices of Manchester University's John Rylands Library, I tried the Inter-university Loans Service and received a copy from the Bodleian Library in Oxford. On reading it, I thought it merited being rescued from an obscurity that had lasted sixty years.

For reasons that I present in my Introduction, I combed through the biographical literature on George Orwell. In an attempt to find out more about Captain Robinson, I enlisted the services of The British Library, The National Army Museum, The Imperial War Museum and The Public Record Office, all in London. While I am grateful to each of these, I should like in particular to thank Paul Carter of the Reference Enquiry Service, Oriental and India Office Collections (The British Library) for the thorough efforts he made on my behalf. On discovering that Robinson's book had been reviewed by George Orwell, I used the excellent services of Manchester's Central Library to locate the review, and I am very grateful to *The Observer* for granting permission to reprint it here (see Appendix). I also want to thank Chris Frape for reminding me to check Frank Kingdon-Ward's work.

I had just completed these researches and written the Introduction to this book, when a book-search dealer telephoned to say that he had at last found a copy of Captain Robinson's book. I asked him how much it would be.

'I think you'd better sit down,' he said.
'OK,' I answered, and sat down.
'Nine hundred pounds.'

I thanked him for his efforts and declined the offer. I wondered why a little book published as late as 1942 should be so scarce and cost so much second-hand. Did the War Office or the Ministry of Information so disapprove of its content, at a time when Burma was being overrun by the Japanese army and the British were in ignominious retreat, that the book was withdrawn? I've tried to find out, but I'm still wondering.

GWA
February 2003

Introduction to the second edition

Herbert Reginald Robinson was born in Stoke Newington, south London, on 6 July, 1896. Seven years later and thousands of miles away, Eric Arthur Blair was born on 25 June, 1903 in Motihari, Bengal, where Eric's father was an official in the Opium Department of the Government of India. As was usual at that time among what were called 'Anglo-Indian' families, Mrs Blair whisked baby Eric off to England, and her husband joined her later. Young Herbert and baby Eric were destined to meet twenty years later in Mandalay, Upper Burma—at that time a part of the British Empire.

When Herbert was still very young, the family moved first to the village of Watton in Norfolk, then to Redhill in Surrey, and finally to Pocklington, a small town near York. Here, he was still in the final year of his schooling when the Great War broke out. Early in the following year he passed the Army's examination for entry to Sandhurst. Almost immediately he was sent to join the Indian Army and attended the Staff College in Quetta. Commissioned on 15 November 1915, he was attached to the 91st Punjab Light Infantry, served in Mesopotamia (now part of Iraq) and was promoted to the rank of Captain on 15 November 1919. The final entry under his name in the Indian Army Lists, on 29 May 1921, records that he was appointed to the Burma Civil Department as assistant commandant in the Military Police, Putao battalion, Konglu—a far-flung outpost in the mountains of north-east Burma. I have not been able to find any records beyond that point.

Back in England, Eric Blair was fast approaching the age of eighteen at the time of Herbert's appointment to the Putao battalion, and the question of Eric's employment arose in family discussions. One biographer (Crick, 1980: 73) has observed:

> The idea of serving in India or Burma. would have come up quite naturally and from the family, especially with his maternal grand-mother still in Mandalay.

Eric arrived in Mandalay on 29 November 1922. Here and in nearby Maymyo he was trained as an assistant superintendent of police (ASP). At the Provincial Police Training School in Mandalay, he was accommodated in the Indian Police Officers' Mess. Another trainee billeted in that same building later explained in his memoirs why one of its bedrooms had long been kept unoccupied. It was because some years earlier a young probationer in that room,

> unable to bear the homesickness which assailed us at all times, shot himself after his first four months. He stretched out on the rug beside his bed, placed the barrel of the shot-gun in his mouth and then pulled the trigger. (Tydd, 1986:15)

The possible effect of this tragic story on ASP Eric Blair will be considered later.

As an Indian Army officer, Robinson had first glimpsed Mandalay back in 1916 but had then been shuttled back and forth across the Bay of Bengal as battalions were being raised and trained for active service in World War I. Not until May 1921 was he sent back to Burma and then he was posted to Konglu (Kawng-lu), an isolated spot in the northernmost tip of Burma. Still a young man, he had tasted the joys of sex for the first time, he tells us, in Mandalay. Here in Konglu he has his second taste with Ayaw, a young and beautiful prisoner who admits murdering her elderly husband. It is not clear whether it was this or some later incident which led to the scandal mentioned by Stansky and Abrahams (see below).

At the beginning of Chapter V, soon after this sexual episode, Robinson met the celebrated plant-hunter Frank Kingdon-Ward, who happened to be returning from a botanical excursion in China at this time and arrived at the far-flung British outpost known as Fort Hertz. In his subsequent account (Kingdon-Ward, 1924:254-7) the botanist describes how he met Robinson:

> ... I wandered past pretty bungalows, and the white hospital, and the post office, and court-house, and came at last to the bungalows of the police officers. And then striding across the compound came an Englishman. It was Captain Robinson, of the Military Police.

We learn that there were normally three white men living in these fairly comfortable surroundings but that

> Robinson did not belong to Fort Hertz really. He was Civil Magistrate and Post Commandant combined at Kawng-lu, which is four days' journey up the hill on the road to the 'Nmai kha; but when the cares of Empire weighed too heavily on his shoulders he drifted down to Fort Hertz for a game of bridge and a drink. The change did him good.

That last observation is not surprising, given Robinson's heavy responsibilities in a spot four days' hard walk from what he would have regarded as 'civilization'. It may well be that Orwell was right when he suggested (see Appendix) that it was this lonely experience which led to Robinson's wish to 'escape from real life' by using opium.

Kingdon-Ward adds another piece of information about Robinson—a rather touching observation, given Herbert's subsequent fate. All the officers loved Fort Hertz, largely because of the good fishing. But this pastime was not for Robinson:

> He did not fish. He had never been known to shoot anything, unless it was sitting still, looking the other way. He did not even collect bugs.

It would soon come to pass that, even when he himself was sitting still and looking the right way, Robinson would prove unable to hit his target fair and square.

It was not until April 1923 that he left the hills and came down to Mandalay, arriving four months later than Eric. Not long afterwards Eric befriended him in spite of the fact that Herbert, according to one account

> after a scandal involving his native mistress, had been cashiered.
> (Stansky and Abrahams, 1972:172)

The possible significance of the scandal, and of the fact that Eric befriended Robinson, will also be considered later. Choosing to stay on in Mandalay, Herbert picked up the opium habit, tried to kick it by becoming a monk, and failed miserably. Another biographer (Shelden, 1991:97) says that Captain Robinson was now 'the most disreputable Englishman in Mandalay' and mentions Herbert's insistence that in his opium trances he had discovered the secret of the universe: 'The banana is great, but the skin is greater'. These trances were the result of frequenting a local opium den. Robinson, in telling us how he constructed his own private 'den', provides another possibly significant detail that will be looked into later.

Robinson had already been repatriated when Eric Blair came home on leave in 1927. Eric was by now sick of his involvement in what he saw as imperialist oppression. Having been one of the oppressors, he explained ten years later, 'I wanted to submerge myself, to get right down among the oppressed'. And he added, 'At that time, failure seemed to me to be the only virtue' (1937:80). In Mandalay's expatriate society, no one could have been a more notorious failure than the disreputable Robinson. Crick (1980:87) remarks sardonically that Blair 'could have earned no bonus marks for knowing such a man as Robinson'.

By the end of 1935 Eric had chosen to be known by the name of George Orwell and had published *Burmese Days*. It is worth considering what effect the above incidents and experiences may have had upon this novel, and also perhaps upon his other works. He had chosen his pseudonym for the publication of *Down and out in Paris and London* (1933), George being a solid English name and Orwell being the name of the river that wound its way to the sea just south of where Eric was now living in Southwold, Sussex. Crick (1980:110) has suggested that even in determining to submerge himself in the underworlds of two capital cities as preparation for this book, Orwell might have been thinking of Robinson's 'attempting to lead the life of a mendicant monk'.

But it is in *Burmese Days* that we are most likely to find echoes of Blair's friendship with Robinson, and I believe there are several. The central character Flory—a misfit like Robinson, and indeed like Blair—has a 'native mistress' who is the cause of his public disgrace. Like Robinson, Flory decides to commit suicide and (also like Robinson) he retires to his bedroom. Before turning his revolver on himself, the despairing Flory shoots his cocker spaniel Flo and then hesitates:

> When she was a yard away he fired, blowing her skull to fragments. Her shattered brain looked like red velvet. Was that what he would look like? The heart then, not the head.

Compare this hesitation with what had happened back in 1925 (two years before Eric left Mandalay for England) when Robinson decided to shoot himself:

> Since I was a very third-rate shot, my first impulse was to bite on the barrel, but a few seconds' reflection was sufficient to change my mind. That would, I thought, result in an unsightly corpse, with the back of the head blown out. The correct way, according to the tenets of common usage, was to fire through the temple. It is strange, is it not, that men should be swayed thus in their final hour?

Did the fact that Robinson at first intended to 'bite on the barrel' indicate that he knew the story of the Training School probationer who 'placed the barrel of the shotgun in his mouth'? Possibly. What can hardly be a coincidence is that both Flory and Robinson worry about what they are going to look like after death. Had this topic cropped up in conversation between Herbert and Eric?

There is also another possible echo of Blair's friendship with Robinson. Flory compares Flo's shattered brain to red velvet, and in his autobiography Robinson tells us that in his own home-made smoking den he installed 'deep red velvet curtains, some nine feet in height, which could be drawn across at will'. This might of course be a simple coincidence; but it could also suggest that Blair had visited Robinson in his 'den' and been confronted with these curtains. Certainly, when Robinson's autobiography was published in 1942, Orwell showed his loyalty to a former friend by reviewing the book in a British national Sunday newspaper, *The Observer* (see Appendix). If he could not bring himself to praise the work, which he considered 'amateurishly written', he at least described it as 'not valueless' and added kindly that those who had known Robinson in the old days would be glad to know that he was still alive and well.

Orwell's review raises again the question of how well Blair knew Robinson—a difficult one to answer because Robinson is very good at not telling us the things that he doesn't want us to know about. For example, there is no mention of being cashiered (if that is what indeed happened). His version is that while up in Putao he applied for a transfer to the North-East Frontier Service in order to avoid being demobilized when the Indian Army shed personnel, but that he later withdrew this application. The next we hear (at the beginning of Ch. X) is of his 'retirement from the Indian Army'. Retirement? Or dishonourable discharge? Significantly, there is no mention of the Police Training School, where he would surely have been billeted if—as he tells us—he was simply awaiting repatriation. There are also further signs of secrecy and concealment, especially at this point in his story. For instance, a few sentences later when describing an evening very soon after his arrival in Mandalay, he says:

> *I was sitting in the Upper Burma Club discussing my plans with two friends, whom I will call the Poet and the Padre.*

Why the need to conceal the identities of these two friends, if all was well? I have no idea who 'the Padre' might have been but, for the following reasons, I suggest that 'the Poet' could well have been Eric Blair.

Even while still at school Eric had seen two of his verses published in local newspapers, and he had presented a special and rather precocious poem to a teenage sweetheart two years his senior (see Crick, 1980:61). It was at that time, he later recalled in one of his 'Why I write' columns, that he 'discovered the joy of mere words', and he continued to write verse of an undistinguished kind in his final years at Eton College. Furthermore, while in Burma he was still conceiving poems, two of which happen to deal with prostitution. The first quoted here is a light, first-person tale with a wry sting in the tail:

ROMANCE
When I was young and had no sense
In far-off Mandalay
I lost my heart to a Burmese girl
As lovely as the day.
Her skin was gold, her hair was jet,
Her teeth were ivory;
I said 'For twenty silver pieces,
Maiden, sleep with me.'
She looked at me, so pure, so sad,
The loveliest thing alive,
And in her lisping, virgin voice,
Stood out for twenty-five.

The other poem, also couched in the first person, is a much darker narrative told by a parson who, when he gets a 'parson's week' (an occasional extended week off duty) guiltily visits a back-street brothel, or perhaps a native mistress. It begins:

THE LESSER EVIL
Empty as death and slow as pain
The days went by on leaden feet;
And parson's week had come again
As I walked down the little street

Just one of the remaining seven verses will suffice to confirm the tone of the poem:

Why did I come, the woman cried
So seldom to her bed of ease?
When I was not, her spirit died
And would I give her ten rupees.
(For the whole poem, see Crick, 1980:92)

What most interests me here is not the question raised by others as to whether or not Blair engaged in such sexual activities—it would be surprising if he did not—but (a) whether Blair was indeed 'the Poet'; and (b) whether, in casting himself as 'parson' in the above poem, Blair was really writing about Robinson's other friend, 'the Padre'—whoever he was.

These questions may prove unanswerable, and much of what I have written above is speculative. But I hope I have said enough to justify this attempt to rescue Robinson's book from oblivion.

References

Crick, B. 1980. *George Orwell: a Life*. London: Seeker and Warburg.

Kingdon-Ward, F. 1924. *From China to Hkamti Long*. London: Edward Arnold.

Orwell, G. 1937. *The Road to Wigan Pier*. London: Victor Gollancz for The Left Book Club.

Shelden, M. 1991. *Orwell: the authorised biography*. Heinemann: London.

Stansky, P. and Abrahams, W. 1972. *The unknown Orwell*. London: Constable.

Tydd, B. 1986. *Peacock Dreams*. London: British Association for Cemeteries in South Asia (BACSA).

Appendix

THE OBSERVER, SUNDAY, 13 SEPTEMBER, 1942

PORTRAIT OF AN ADDICT
'A Modern de Quincey'
By Captain H.R. Robinson
(Harrap, 8s. 6d. net)

By GEORGE ORWELL

Unjustified in other ways, the title of this book does have the excuse that its author, like de Quincey, is very much interested in his own reactions as an opium-smoker. An officer of the Indian Army, seconded to the Burma Military Police, he was axed in 1923 and settled down for a couple of years in Mandalay, where he devoted himself almost exclusively to smoking opium, though he did have a brief interlude as a Buddhist monk and made unsuccessful efforts to float a gold mine and run a car-hiring business. After a short visit to England, during which he tried quite vainly to cure himself of the opium habit, he returned to Mandalay, and on being arrested for debt attempted suicide—a ghastly failure, for instead of blowing out his brains as he had intended he merely blew out both eyeballs, blinding himself for life.

* * *

This bald outline of the facts does not do injustice to Captain Robinson's book, which, in spite of the long passages devoted to the delights of opium, leaves a great deal unexplained. Those who knew the author in Mandalay in 1923 were completely unable to understand why a young, healthy and apparently happy man should give himself up to such a debilitating and—in a European—unusual vice, and on this point the book throws no further light. Captain Robinson merely explains that some night in Mandalay he happened to see some Chinese smoking their opium, decided to try what it was like, and thereafter became a habitual opium-smoker. Some other reason for wanting to escape from real life there must have been. It is never mentioned, but the clue is possibly to be found in the earlier part of the book, which describes Captain Robinson's adventures as a frontier magistrate among the little-known tribes in the north-east corner of Burma.

* * *

What are the pleasures of opium? Like other pleasures, they are, unfortunately, indescribable. It is easier to describe the miseries which the smoker suffers when deprived of his drug: he is seized with feverish restlessness, then with violent fits of yawning, and finally howls like a dog, a noise so distressing that when an opium-smoker is imprisoned in an Indian jail he is usually, quite illegally, given diminishing doses to keep him quiet. Like many other smokers, Captain Robinson felt himself, while under the influence of the drug, to be possessed of almost divine wisdom. He was aware that he not only knew the secret of the Universe, but had reduced this secret to a single sentence, which he was unfortunately never able to recall when he woke up. One night, so as to make sure of remembering it, he took a pad and pencil when he lay down to smoke. The sentence in which all wisdom was contained turned out to be: 'the banana is great, but the skin is greater'.

* * *

This book is a small but not valueless contribution to the literature of opium. It is amateurishly written, but its facts are truthful. The description of the attempted suicide is worth the rest of the book put together. It is profoundly interesting to know what the mind can still contain in the face of apparently certain death—interesting to know, for instance, that a man can be ready to blow his brains out but anxious to avoid a disfiguring wound. Those who knew Captain Robinson in the old days will be glad to receive this evidence of his continued existence, and to see the photograph of him at the beginning of the book, completely cured of the opium habit and apparently well-adjusted and happy, in spite of his blindness.

Postscript

The writer whose review first drew my attention to Robinson's book, Phil Baker of *The Guardian* (London), is able to close the story for us. He reports that Robinson became a hospital physiotherapist in South London, and worked until his retirement in the 1960s. In March 1965, however, forty years after his first attempt in Burma, he finally killed himself.

GWA

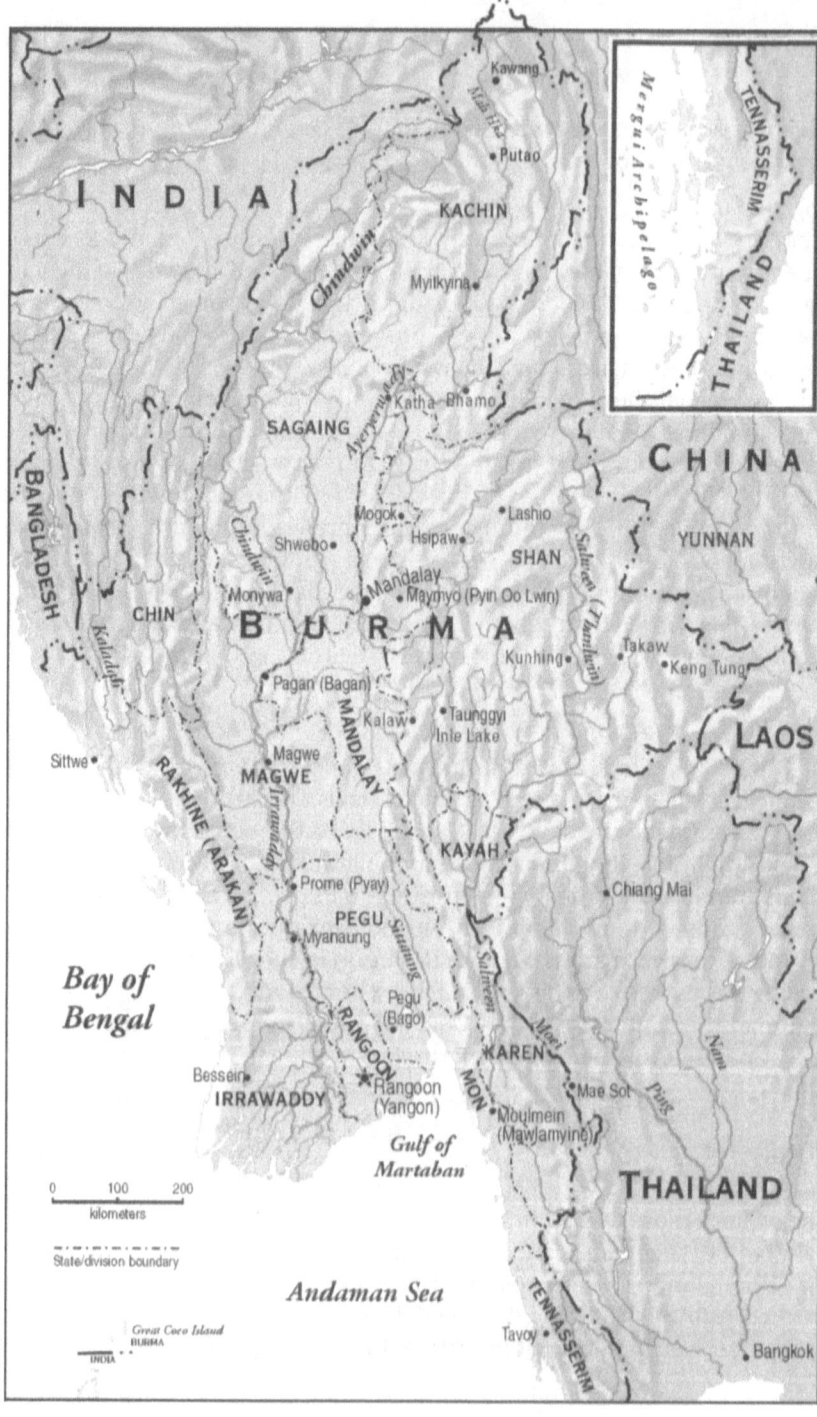

Preface

In placing on record in these pages certain events in my life I am actuated, in the main, by a feeling of detached interest. Time and circumstance have enabled me to view the past as though it were the mapped-out record of a journey. The course this journey eventually took was governed by two things: forces outside my control, and a few important decisions of my own. The former were in their way immutable; yet, nevertheless, they had the appearance of being dependent on the latter. There were certain times in my pilgrimage through life when I had a definite choice between two roads, and the nature of the external circumstances which I encountered seemed to be determined by the route selected. Yet, after all, was it as simple as all that? No, I do not think this is all. We are irresistibly impelled by powers beyond our comprehension from the time of our birth, and, though later we may in some measure steer our own course, the general direction is laid down for us before we are able to have any say in the matter.

I do not offer these thoughts as an excuse for the events and actions hereinafter related. It may be true, and I believe that it is so, that no act can be performed without its repercussions on the lives of other people. However, so long as such repercussions are not a hindrance to the evolution of the soul of any other man, I do not hold myself answerable to anyone but myself. If my life has been a failure I am prepared to accept the full responsibility, and I have no desire to seek salvation through the sufferings of others. What I have done I have done, and the censure or praise of the world is of little moment to me. I have been down in the mud, but my experiences there have not been without value. There are, stored away in my heart, one or two memories the fragrance of which is ever with me, and, if only for these, I would not have had it otherwise.

H. R. R.

Foreword

VISIONS OF THE PAST
(1896-1914)

I see a straight road, running from left to right upon my map. Towards the left it fades into the mist of forgotten centuries, but it becomes clearer and more personal to me where it is crossed by a definite line marking the close of the Victorian era. The path allows of no deviation, either to the right or to the left, and willy-nilly I must travel along it.

In the first short stretch, up to the line of demarcation, two visions float up to me.

The first is very faint. I see myself as a small boy, perched high on a man's shoulder, outside a sweet-shop in the village of Watton, in Norfolk, waving a flag as soldiers march down the village street.

The second is clearer. It is Sunday morning in the same village, and this same small boy has just returned home from Sunday school. Something he has heard that morning has evidently impressed him, for he is engaged in crucifying a frog on the door of the stable-yard. He is not naturally cruel, but merely curious.

Some ten years have passed, and I am still being hustled along that straight and rather monotonous road. Here another very clear vision emerges. It is of a large school at Redhill, in Surrey, and the boy is monitor in charge of the Chapel. This is his first Sunday in his new position, and I see him sitting cross-legged on the vestry floor in front of the cupboard containing the Communion vessels. He has to set out the things for the Communion, but, not yet having been confirmed, he does not know what to do. Silver chalice, cups, plates, a little lace-edged cloth, two or three squares of cardboard covered with silk, a slice of bread, and a bottle of wine: all are spread out before him. He translates the Latin words on the bottle ... 'Sacred wine.' He draws the cork and sniffs. It smells good. He wonders what it tastes like, but ... no, it is sacred wine. Something dreadful might happen to little boys who did things like that. He replaces the cork and turns to the bread. This holds no terrors for him. Had he not seen the cook cut it off the loaf that very morning? As he chews the crusts he divides the remainder into little cubes with a cutter provided for the purpose. Again his eye wanders to the bottle. Will anything really happen if he has just one sip? He reaches for it, and a funny feeling runs down his spine as he puts it to his lips. Sacred wine! What will happen? Everlasting damnation? He gulps down a mouthful, puts down the bottle, and waits.... Nothing happens; nothing, except a very pleasant warm feeling inside his tummy. The Rubicon is crossed. He takes a longer sip, and the world seems very good to him.

I must pass over the rest of that vision in a few brief words. The boy did himself well in the vestry that morning, and, with some vague remembrances about the Last Supper, laid out the Communion vessels on the altar accordingly. In the middle was a piece of silk-covered cardboard on which stood a silver dish containing the bread. To the right of this was a knife and to the left a neatly folded napkin. The silver cup and the flagon containing what was left of the wine were standing in the place where he was accustomed to find his own tea mug at breakfast-time. It was all very simple, and he was really astonished at the glare of anger which the headmaster cast in his direction on arrival in Chapel, but, thanks to the wine, the boy was feeling on top of the world.

There was one master in the choir who seldom appeared to have any money for the collection, and was wont to wave away the Chapel Monitor during the offertory. He had kept the boy in that week for some trifling misdemeanour—I believe he had been found making geometrical figures by joining the drops of spittle which the same master was apt to shower on the front desks during a maths lesson. This morning the boy failed to notice the surreptitious waves of the master's hand, and, standing with, downcast eyes, offertory bag in hand, he shamed the master before the whole school.

As that rather regrettable vision fades I see the same boy, now mangrown, standing in that same attitude in the burning heat of a Mandalay morning. It is a begging-bowl which he, bareheaded, bare-foot, and clad in the yellow robe of a Buddhist priest, now holds out. His eyes are still downcast, and he still is filled with an insatiable curiosity.

There were objects even at this early age which seemed to draw my mind towards the east. In my home there hung two old prints—one of the fort at Agra, the other of the fort at Allahabad. They had a strange fascination for me. It was curious, too, that, although the family had no previous connexion with the East, my eldest brother should, in 1912, enter the Indian Police, and that the rest of his career in that service should be spent in the United Provinces of Agra and Oudh.

At this period it was customary for me to be sent to spend my Easter holidays at a little village in Normandy. I stayed at the Presbytery, and, in order to please the old curé, attended the Roman Catholic church on

Sundays. It is in this setting that another vision comes back to me. Again it is Sunday morning, and this same boy is seated in the curé's own stall, while the old priest wanders about, cuffing the choir-boys. Bread is being passed round the congregation. No dainty cubes these, but healthy slices which he had seen the *bonne* cutting from a long loaf that very morning. He takes a portion, but, not feeling hungry, passes it over the back of his stall to a peasant girl. He is waiting for something, and is conscious of a not unpleasant tingle of anticipatory dread. Only that very morning the *bonne* had solemnly warned him that he must keep his eyes closed during the elevation of the Host. If he looked on the Host, she said, he would be struck blind. The anxiously awaited moment arrived. Slowly he opened his eyes, and saw the old priest holding up something in a silver casket. The palms of the boy's hands were sweating with apprehensive excitement, but...nothing happened. He could still see. I do not know which was uppermost in his mind—relief or disappointment. Seeds of scepticism were certainly beginning to take root there, but they were untarnished by traces of cynicism; he was only very, very curious.

Some years later—September 1914. Pocklington School, East Yorkshire. The last vision of my school days conjures up the mathematics master exclaiming: 'But, my dear boy, the War will be over by Christmas. Don't you be such a fool. Buckle down to your maths, and you'll be up at Cambridge next year. You can take it from me—it will all be over by Christmas.'

Now at last I came to the end of that long, undeviating road, to the point where the first fork was to afford me a first opportunity to use my freedom of choice. The war not being over by Christmas, I decided to enlist in the Public Schools Battalion of the Royal Fusiliers. Shortly after Christmas I was walking to the battalion headquarters to enlist, when a placard happened to catch my eye. An army entrance examination for Sandhurst was due to be held very shortly, and applications were invited. I filled in the forms, attended at a crammer's establishment in Chancery Lane for a month, and on April 17, 1915, in company with forty-nine other gentlemen cadets, embarked at Tilbury on the s.s. Egypt, *en route* for the Staff College at Quetta and the East.

Chapter I

THE ROAD TO MANDALAY

The railway journey from Karachi to Quetta is not, perhaps, the best introduction to India, more especially when it is undertaken in the month of May. The colourful glamour of the East was not apparent, and in its place appeared a vista of desert and barren hills, sweltering heat, and very little shade. Quetta did little to mitigate this disappointment. Its lay-out was too austere for a young mind, inclined towards sensuousness, to appreciate. It was not until later that I was to recognize its peculiar attraction, and to realize what a tonic a spell on the Frontier can be to one whose health and virility have been sapped by overlong service in the plains.

Shortly before the conclusion of the course a notice was circulated to the effect that, should the cadets have any preference, they might apply for a particular regiment, and, where possible, they would be posted accordingly. Some of the cadets had family connexions in certain units, but for me there were no such ties or attachments. Apart from the fact that I could not afford to join the Cavalry and had no desire to be posted to a Pioneer regiment, it mattered little where I went, but there was one factor to be taken into account—the locality in which the regiment happened to be stationed at that time. I had grown weary of scrambling up and down these bare, rocky hills, and my soul thirsted for a more fertile and colourful landscape.

My eye wandered over the map. There were many places in the plains of India which appeared to be as flat as the proverbial pancake, but I was not wholly satisfied as to their verdancy. My eye crossed the Bay of Bengal to Burma. A few lines of a half-forgotten poem began to tiptoe through my head: 'I've a neater, sweeter maiden in a cleaner, greener land.' Mandalay, Mandalay! I eagerly scrutinized the map, and found that this place fulfilled my requirements. True, there was a hill outside the walls of the old fort, but another reference to a book on Burma informed me that it was almost completely covered with pagodas. Well, Mandalay it should be. A glance at the Indian Army List told me that there were two Indian Infantry units stationed there. One was a Pioneer regiment, the other was the 91st Punjab Light Infantry. My choice was made. A few weeks later, in the middle of

November 1915, I left Quetta for Calcutta *en route* for Rangoon and... Mandalay.

During the cold weather Calcutta is a delightful, if rather expensive, city. I was to become better acquainted with it in later years, but on this, my first visit, I was vouchsafed only a fleeting glimpse of its many attractions. There was time enough, however, for a very susceptible newly commissioned subaltern to fall in love with a pretty face, and it was with feelings akin to despair that I boarded the steamer at the Outram Ghat. Little did I realize then how before very long my heart was to be captivated by the soul of a people.

Many times have I crossed the Bay of Bengal—in the old boats, where the first-class cabins were over the propellers, and in the more modern ships—but always one seems to enter the Rangoon river at daybreak. I was on deck early that first morning as we entered the Delta, and I experienced the first faint tuggings at my heart-strings that each such repeated spectacle was to strengthen, until it finally became for me the epitome of a homecoming. There are, no doubt, many more beautiful sights in the world, but I would give them all for another glimpse of those flat, mud-covered banks with the tops of the little white pagodas peeping above the mists, and as we approach nearer Rangoon the glory of the rays of the rising sun striking the golden *hti* of the great Shwe Dagon Pagoda. And so I came, at last, to Burma... and my destiny.

Mandalay was far from any front, and it seemed hard to realize that there was a war on. Life flowed very smoothly and pleasantly in the old fort. Early-morning parade, breakfast, orderly-room, tiffin, a sleep in the afternoon, tea, polo, the Club, dinner, and bed... what more could one want? There were many things to be learned, including the fact (which always stuck in my gullet) that 'Ignorance of orders is no excuse for neglect of duty.' I also took to heart many things which, but for an innate, simple credulity, I should have questioned. For instance, a senior officer once told me that, should I ever be attacked by a hamadryad (king cobra), the best thing to do was to catch it by the tail and run. A few years later I did meet a very large hamadryad, face to face, in the early morning as I was rounding a bend in a very narrow mountain path. I do not know which of us was the more astonished. There was no room to pass with comfort, and as we both stopped dead his evil, swaying head was not more than six or eight feet from my face and nearly on the same level. I carried a swagger-cane and a small-calibre automatic, but both were useless. I did *not* catch hold of his tail and run. I couldn't have moved to have saved my life. I just stood there in a cold sweat of terror while he inspected me, and then he must have heard the clink of my pony's stirrups as it was being led along in the rear by my orderly, for he turned aside and glided down the mountain-side at an incredible speed. No, I do not like snakes, and yet every morning before parade I drove down to the bathing-pool of the old palace for an early dip. It was a rectangular stone tank overhung with trees, and as I slipped into the enclosure I sometimes saw three or four snakes glide off the sides into the water. Diving in at the deep end, I would swim furiously up the length of the pool and emerge the other end very much refreshed. One morning, however, as I swam I felt something tap-tap-tapping against my thigh. I made for the side like a rocket and never went in that tank again.

Well, we all learn by experience, and I had many things to learn. One such experience had to do with fire-arms. Early in 1916 I was returning from Poona, where I had been attending a physical training course. In the same carriage was a friend of mine, an officer in the Gurkhas, and as we talked I took out a revolver and, pointing it at his stomach, pulled the trigger five times in succession. I knew it was not loaded, as I had spent the previous evening in a canoe on the river having pot-shots at the flying foxes, and had expended all my ammunition. However, acting on some vagrant whim, I tired of pressing the trigger at my friend's tummy and pointed the revolver at the ceiling lamp. There was a deafening explosion as a bullet went through the roof. It was a terrible experience for both of us, for, rotten shot though I may be, I could not have missed him. Of course, there was an explanation but no excuse. My bearer, having found a loose round, had put it in the revolver, and, owing to its peculiar mechanism, that chamber became the last one to be fired. It taught me the necessary lesson, however, and ever after that, if anyone pointed a gun at me, even though I knew it was unloaded, I had a nasty sensation in the pit of my stomach, and expressed my feelings in no uncertain voice.

A pleasant spell of recruiting duty in the Punjab was brought to an abrupt end that summer by the news that the regiment had been ordered to Mesopotamia. On my return to Mandalay I found that the old, pleasant, lazy life had given place to great bustle and activity. Every one was delighted at the news and none more than myself, but my delight was tinged with a certain anxiety. How should I stand up to this baptism of fire? How should I feel 'when the guns begin to shoot'? I was considering this one morning when in charge of a party of men on the musketry range. Suddenly an idea occurred to me. Telling the Indian officer to carry on, I walked up the side of the range until I was within a hundred yards of the butts. Removing my helmet, I proceeded to crawl on my stomach, taking advantage of every bit of cover, until I was in the middle of the range, and there I squatted with my back to a scrubby bush. And then the fun began. You see, I had forgotten there were some of my recruits on the firing line. Bullets whizzed past my ears, others plonked in the dust around me. It was terrible. I dared not move and had to wait till the 'Cease fire' was sounded. Of course, it was very foolhardy of me, but I had been curious to know what it felt like to be under fire, and... I had found out.

It was on a sweltering day in August 1916 that the regiment, headed by its band, marched through the streets of Rangoon to embark on the troopship which was to take us round the southern point of India to Basra. They were pre-War soldiers, those Mohammedans, Sikhs, and Dogras, and their full-throated shouts of 'Raj Ki Jai' ('Victory to the Empire') could not but stir a feeling of pride in their latest war-baby of a subaltern. Be that as it may, this embarkation left me with the same pang of parting that I was always to experience when leaving Burma.

Mesopotamia was to hold very little attraction for me. Sand and heat, heat and sand; it was the antithesis of Burma, and, in my opinion, well deserved the Tommy's description of 'miles and miles of sweet F.A.' It is not a pleasant place even when there is no fighting in progress.

It was during my short period of service there that I witnessed what I believe and hope was one of the last floggings in the Indian Army. The accused, a Sikh sepoy, had been posted as sentry over the mess stores. During the night he had opened a bottle of brandy, and, in a subsequent fit of martial emotion, had proceeded to stab all the tinned goods with his bayonet. The sentence of the court-martial was thirty lashes to be administered before the regiment. I shall never forget that sight.

The regiment was formed up on three sides of a square, the fourth side of which was occupied by an A.T. cart. To one wheel of this cart the prisoner, naked except for a loin-cloth, was bound, his arms and legs making a St Andrew's Cross. Close by stood the Colonel, the Adjutant, the Medical Officer, and a British Provost Sergeant. The sentence having been promulgated, the sergeant drew the cat-o'-nine-tails from a bag. The Adjutant counted each stroke as it came down on the man's back. It was not a pleasant sight. I was in front of my company and could see the quiver of the man's back as the lashes fell. During the first half-dozen there was a deathly silence broken only by the clear voice of the Adjutant and the swish and plunk of the cat. Then the prisoner began to hurl abuse at the sergeant, who, unmoved, continued to draw the tails of the cat through the palm of his left hand before raising his arm for the next stroke. Distraught with the pain, the man called on his countrymen to come to his aid. There was a clatter of rifle behind me, but it was only a young recruit who had fallen down in a faint. I was feeling pretty rotten myself, but managed to stick it out. 'Nineteen, twenty, twenty-one...' It seemed interminable, yet there was no movement in the ranks, except for an odd recruit here and there who had to fall out.

I saw the man later as he lay, face downward, in the M.O.'s tent. His back was a ghastly mess. Well, of course, active service *is* active service, and it might well have been that such wanton destruction of food-supplies might have spelt starvation to other men; but, still... the shame, the degradation, the brutality; of the whole affair.... Personally I would have preferred a nice, quiet, quick shooting at dawn.

However, I was not destined to stay in Mesopotamia long. Towards the end of the year I contracted dysentery and was eventually evacuated to India.

Chapter II

A BURMESE INTERLUDE

Shortly after my discharge from hospital I rejoined the regimental depot at Rangoon, and then followed a year of very pleasant existence. It was during this period that I began to be absorbed by the beauty and charm of Burma and the Burmese. To me Rangoon cannot be visualized without the background of the Shwe Dagon Pagoda. The golden, tapering edifice, surmounted by the jewelled *hti*, stands on high ground and dominates the city. It was my custom in the evening to take a canoe from the Boat Club and paddle among the less-frequented backwaters of the palm-fringed lakes. The marvellous sunsets and the faint whisper of the little bells on the *hti* held a fascination for me that was morbidly depressing. Being very young, I wanted to die, but contented myself with writing verses:

> *The Setting Sun!*
> *Reluctantly it sinks into the West,*
> *Shedding its glorious multi-coloured rays*
> *Upon a world oppressed.*
> *'Tis then I long, dreading the future days,*
> *Slowly to enter the Eternal Rest,*
> *A Setting Sun.*

And, had I but known it, there were to be future days in this beautiful land which I should have good cause to dread.

But, thank God, I did not know, and meanwhile I was young, and everything in life was good. And so at other times I would join a congenial party of young officers and after dinner drive down to a small wooden house near Monkey Point to drink beer with Auntie and her little ones. A curious place this, with an atmosphere all its own. Auntie was half Burmese and half Indian (Zerbadi), and was middle-aged, fat, and jolly. She had been a teacher in a Catholic school, but the pay had been very inadequate and the work hard. So one day she failed to turn up, and three or four of her prettiest pupils were also found to be missing. And here they were, living in sin, but, believe it or not, thoroughly enjoying themselves. You see, Auntie took great care of her little ones. They were very religious.

There were many texts round the walls of the rooms, and none of them appeared to find it at all disconcerting to know that 'The Lord watcheth beside thy bed.' It was all so gloriously naïve and simple, and a visit there never produced that guilty feeling such as you might experience after a night at those plush-covered hell-haunts in Kariah Lane, at Calcutta, or Grant Road, in Bombay.

Early in 1918 I left Burma and was not destined to return for three years. At this period of the War many new battalions were being raised in India, and it was to one of these, the 2/90th Punjabis, that I was transferred. The battalion was stationed at Dhond, a desolate railway junction, near Poona. With the exception of one Mohammedan company, its composition was Hindu, including Sikhs, Brahmins, Punjabi Hindus, and Ahirs. We were still engaged in training this new battalion when the Armistice was declared. But it was not until 1921, after a spell on the North-west Frontier, where a spot of bother had occurred, that the battalion was sent to Kirkee, near Poona, for disbandment. I had been a witness of its formation, and as adjutant it fell to my lot to carry out its final dispersion.

While in Waziristan I had put my name down for the Burma Military Police, and shortly before the last draft left Poona to return to their units I received my transfer orders.

Now, apart from the duties assigned to it by the Government of India, the Burma Military Police performs a very special duty in the lives of Indian Army officers under field rank. Army bankers in India are the most lenient of financiers, but a time does come when the amoeba-like growth of an overdraft will cause even him to protest. It is then that the owner of the overdraft applies for transfer to the B.M.P. This force, part foot and part mounted infantry, is under the command of officers seconded from the Indian Army for that purpose. The pay and allowances, are good, and there are, in addition, many opportunities and awards for the passing of examinations in the many languages spoken throughout the country.

I arrived back in Rangoon in May, and found that I had been posted to the Shwebo battalion, with my headquarters at Katha, a small township on the Irrawaddy. I had five other posts under my supervision, and it was my custom to visit them periodically when funds were low and circumstances made it necessary. T.A. (Travelling Allowance) is one of the main arteries of a Military Police Officer's existence. They are the two sweetest-sounding letters in the alphabet to him. But its appeal is even more universal. It is the one human connecting link, the lowest common factor, as it were, between the highest executive officers and the lowest-grade baboos in the Government of India.

Life at Katha was very pleasant. Battalion headquarters were at Shwebo, some miles down the railway, and the battalion commandant did not trouble me overmuch. My wooden bungalow overlooked the quarter-guard and the lines, and when feeling particularly indolent I could supervise the morning parades from my upper veranda as I sipped my morning tea. Sometimes I watched the yellow-robed *hpongyis*, begging-bowl in hand, on their morning rounds. They looked so extraordinarily serene and the laity so absurdly happy. I felt that there must be some singular quality in Buddhism which left those brows smooth and untouched by theological wrinkles.

These halcyon days came to an end at last, for in November of that same year, 1921, I was transferred to the Putao Battalion on the North-east Frontier.

1. Captain Robinson in 1919

Chapter III

THE NORTH-EAST FRONTIER

It was on the 1st of December that I set out from Myitkyina, the rail-head in the north of Burma, for my 250-mile march to my new post at Konglu, in the Futao District. Behind me straggled a line of mules, bearing on their patient backs provisions and necessaries for my next twelve months of existence. The rest of the party consisted of my Burmese servant, my Gurkha orderly, and a band of blue-clad, impassive, but vociferously eloquent Chinese muleteers. I had to adjust the length of my marches to the pace of the mules, and on this account it was seldom that I could cover each day more than a single stage, a matter of ten to fifteen miles.

It was soon apparent to me that I was entering a different world from any in which I had previously lived. Mountains, jungle, and rushing rivers—in contour similar to the North-west Frontier, but—oh! how different. The North-west Frontier was like a wrinkled, wizened, dried-up old hag watching over her hardy sons, who seemed to thrive on the meagre sustenance derived from her withered breasts. But here was a voluptuous, full-blooded matron, the milk oozing from her over-abundant breasts till the very air seemed fetid with the rank odour of wasted fertility. This feeling of uncontrolled genesis in nature was, at times, overpowering, and I well remember a glade, just outside Putao itself, where my senses would never fail to stir as if in the presence of some vast cosmic rape.

The road, barely wide enough for two mules to pass, was cut out of the sides of the hills and wandered up, down, and around in a more or less northerly direction. On the right could be caught occasional glimpses of the Mali Hka, one of the main sources of the great Irrawaddy. On the other side of the river lay the Triangle, an expanse of tribal territory not, at that time, under British control. The Government rest-houses at the end of each stage were usually situated on a hill, and on rising early for the next day's march I was always greeted by a sight which never failed to thrill me. A vast sea of white mist, filling all the valleys, would be stretched out before me, and from this sea would rise, as it were, little islands of jungle-covered slopes crowned, maybe, by the long thatched huts of a Kachin village. It was difficult to leave this beautiful scene, glittering in the morning sunlight, and to plunge down the steep path into the very heart of the mist where everything was dark and damp and dripping; where long, snake-like creepers hung in festoons from the trees, and even the sight of brilliant orchids only served to emphasize the inherent unhealthiness of the place.

I arrived at Konglu on Christmas Eve and found that my new home was situated on the top of a hill some 6,000 feet high. My quarters, which were built on a level space cut into the hillside, consisted of a three-roomed hut made of roughly dressed planks and thatched with a leaf called 'tingolap'. The Military Police post was higher up the hill, and the bungalow and offices of the Civil Magistrate a hundred yards or so below me.

Konglu was actually a two-man post—a Civil Officer in charge of all civil matters and a Military Police officer in charge of the defence of the post and other matters pertaining thereto.

Except for the first few weeks, however, I was there alone and was the sole representative of both the civil and military authorities. Naturally, being in such a position, I had many designations from which to choose, and this was very convenient at times. On returning from a tour of inspection of my district I, as Assistant Commandant of Burma Military Police, would submit my claim for travelling allowance to myself, as Assistant Superintendent of the North-east Frontier. I would then take the document, duly sanctioned, passed, and signed, to the Quarter-guard, where, as Sub-Treasury Officer, I would carefully scrutinize it and pay out the money. And had I cared to embezzle the Government funds, who was there to say me nay? Remember, I was the Sub-divisional Judge, and—well, Delhi was a very long way off.

Those first twelve months at Konglu were interesting, if rather lonely. Apart from an occasional visit to Putao, the District headquarters, I never saw another white man and rarely spoke my own tongue. But there was plenty of work to do, and there were the natives and their languages to be studied. Several tribes came under my jurisdiction, and each had its own peculiar language. Kachins, Nungs, Marus, and Lisus—they had one thing in common: there was no written language, and the majority of them were Animists. They had a peculiar tradition to explain these two things, and also the fact that they were very poor. In the beginning, they would say, the Great Chief called all the tribes of the earth together to a meeting at Mandalay. He then distributed among them their systems of writing. To some he gave them inscribed on palm-leaves; the Kachins received theirs on skins. But on the long march home the Kachins got so hungry that they were forced to boil the skins and eat them. Hence they have no written language. Once again the Great Chief summoned the tribes, and this time he was distributing worldly goods. The Chinese and the Burmese had brought large baskets, but the Kachins had none. Consequently the Chinese and the Burmese went away well laden, and the simple-minded tribesmen could only take what they could carry in their hands. On receiving a third summons, however, they decided not to be outdone this time and brought many baskets with them. But this time the Great Chief was handing out gods. The Chinese and the Burmese, who apparently had some inside information on these matters, came empty-handed and received only one god each. The rest of the stock was piled into the baskets which the Kachins had so carefully brought. The load was heavy and the way home across the mountains very long. Who can blame them if, when fording a river or threading their way through the jungle, they surreptitiously removed a god and dropped it by the wayside? And so, all over this part of the world you will come across simple little offerings of food and flowers at the foot of some tree or, maybe, at the crossing of some stream, thus marking the places where very long ago the gods themselves were dropped.

My personal establishment at Konglu was simple, if somewhat varied. Apart from my personal servants, I kept ducks, hens, pigeons, five monkeys, and a bear. The monkeys were never tied up, but had the free run of the house and compound by day, only being shut up at nightfall. They became very tame, and, though they had been brought to me straight from the jungle, I never had any trouble in taming them. Every day they would queue up at the cook-house for their bowls of boiled rice, and it was on one of these occasions that an incident occurred which will illustrate their affection for me. I had gone into the cook-house to discuss certain matters with the cook, when, after a time, I became conscious of something tapping on my leg. I then heard the mewing of a monkey, and, looking down, I saw that I had been standing on the hind-paw of one of my favourites. He was looking up at me and tapping my calf with his front paw, but, though in evident distress, he made no attempt to bite me.

The bear was presented to me by some Kachins who had killed the mother in their paddy-fields. He was black with a yellowish-white collar, and, when I first had him, was about the same size as the Teddy bears sold in English shops. He too had the run of the place and would turn up at the cook-house with the monkeys for this daily allowance of rice. The little beggar would stuff himself until his tummy bulged like a balloon. Then, waddling outside into the sunlight, he would stand up rather unsteadily on his hind-feet and growl. This was the chance for which the monkeys were waiting. One of them would rush up behind him and push him over. Grunting and growling with rage, the little bear would turn on his tormenters, but, of course, it was hopeless.

The monkeys were constantly in mischief, and one of their favourite pastimes was to rob my hen-house. On hearing a frightful disturbance coming from this quarter I would look down, and then round the corner of the hut would appear four monkeys, in single file, walking on their hind-legs, and under each arm would be tucked an egg. These they would carry to a secluded spot, where they would drop them and lick up the contents. It was difficult to be angry with them.

You may have noticed that I have only mentioned four of the monkeys as taking part in these egg-stealing raids. The fifth monkey, a beautifully furred female, was blind. She had walked straight into the circle of my camp fire one evening when I was out on tour. How she lost her sight I do not know. How she had survived in the jungle is inexplicable. Men and the smell of man meant nothing to her; her sense of touch was her only safeguard. If I held a rope in front of her she would climb without fear, and it was only when she touched my hand that she would realize the presence of a man. Her eyes looked perfectly normal, but, though she got to know me well, she was never as tame as the rest. Poor little thing! She led a rather exciting existence in the company of her four somewhat amorous boy friends. No wonder that she used to come to me for a little peace and quiet.

The pigeons too were tame and very prolific, but their numbers were kept down by the marauding raids of the monkeys and my fondness for pigeon-pie. I did not shoot them with gun or rifle. For one thing that would have been expensive, and, for another, as Kingdon-Ward has remarked of me in one of his books, I could not shoot anything unless it were sitting down and looking the other way. This was true, and all the jungle seemed to know it. I remember one day, when on tour, rounding a bend in a path and coming unexpectedly on a barking-deer feeding by the side of the road. It was not more than twenty yards away, but I missed.

In the case of the pigeons, however, I emulated the sparrow and shot them with a bow and arrow. The Kachin cross-bow is a powerful weapon, shooting slim bamboo arrows with considerable accuracy. When these are tipped with poison they can account for even tiger or bear. My first attempts at this novel method of game-hunting were a grisly failure. Waiting until the selected bird had settled on the roof of my hut, I took careful aim, and the arrow pierced it clean through from front to back. To my amazement, the pigeon flew off and continued to fly about for several hours, transfixed through the body by my little arrow. Later I learned to shoot them sideways, so that the arrow, passing through the body, neatly pinned the wings to the birds' sides, preventing them from flying. Whatever may be said about my marksmanship with a gun or a rifle, I was something of an expert with a cross-bow by the time I left Konglu.

Another welcome addition to my larder was obtained when Chinese came in from over the border to sell their sheep. I would purchase an animal, usually a male, as my men refused to eat female flesh, and decapitate it with one cut of dah. The heart, liver, and kidneys I would keep for my own consumption, passing the meat on to the men. There is very little trouble about caste rules when dealing with Gurkhas, and I got on excellently well with my seventy-five Military Policemen. It was through them that I was initiated into the gruesome art of decapitating any animal up to a water-buffalo with a single sweep from a dah or a kukri. I was first a witness of this feat at their feast of Dussehra in 1922. It was a great occasion, and I was the principal, and only, guest. An enormous buffalo with wide-spreading horns had been purchased for the sacrifice, and a specially selected Gurkha had been practising with an outsized kukri for some days beforehand. You see, the ultimate fertility of the crops depends on the ability of this man to decapitate the buffalo with one strike. On the morning of the day appointed the whole garrison assembled on the parade ground. In the centre had been erected the sacrificial post to which was fastened by his horns the immense water-buffalo. Round the post in a ring were tethered several goats, and outside these a larger ring of pumpkins with sticks for legs and horns. The signal was given, and the selected Gurkha walked round the outer circle severing each pumpkin with his kukri. The goats were then dealt with in a similar manner, and then came the great moment. Taking his specially prepared kukri, he raised it above his head, and with one quick, strong sweep cut off the head of the buffalo. Great rejoicings followed as the bleeding carcass was hauled round the post so as to encircle it with the blood of the sacrifice. Meanwhile the hero of the hour was led up to me so that I might tie round his head the white turban of honour. It was all very interesting, and so were the feast and dancing which followed. The Gurkhas are very fond of a convivial evening and make very importunate hosts. Can I be blamed, therefore, if I fell in love temporarily with one of the dancing-girls, only to discover, to the delight of all present, that the enchanting little houri was really none other than the post bugler dressed up for the occasion?

Yes, they were very pleasant, those early days on my hill-top in Konglu. The sun rose and set on a landscape vastly different from that of Burma proper, but it had a charm and a sadness all its own. As I sat in the evening outside my little bungalow my eyes would travel over ridge after ridge of virgin-clad hills to where, in the far distance, the snow-capped peaks of the Himalayas would glisten in the fading light. I knew that my duties would take me to those distant mountains, and I wondered what fresh experiences awaited me in this land of jungles and mists and everlasting hills.

Chapter IV

A HIMALAYAN LOVE INTERLUDE

I was seated one morning in the little room in my bungalow which served me as a court-house. It was the time of the rains, and the mists had forsaken the valleys and were swirling round the hill-tops. The drip-drip of the rain on the thatched roof formed a soft but ever-present accompaniment to the monotonous droning of an old Kachin who was squatting on the floor in front of my table. A dah was slung round his shoulder, and from a monkey-skin bag he had produced a little bundle of twigs, each about an inch in length. As he told his tale he laid these twigs down on the floor in front of him until, with his concluding words, the last twig completed the line. These little twigs were his script, and with their aid he could produce his tale of woe, and always the same story, at any time. Without them he would have been lost. He was a peculiar old man with an even more peculiar tale. Years ago he had been mixed up in a blood-feud and had received a gash across the face from a dah which had cut away half of his lower jaw. The interior of his mouth was a sickening sight, but I forced myself to keep my eyes fixed on him as he made his complaint. It appeared that he had sold a water-buffalo with a white tail to a neighbour, unaware, until the deal had been completed, that the spirit of his father had decided to take up residence in that very white tail of that very buffalo. He now wanted to get the animal back so that the spirit of his ancestor should be under his personal care. The present owner would not part with it and had already declined my suggestion of an amputation. It was all very difficult. As I considered the situation there rose a sudden buzz of excited talk from the little knot of natives sheltering under the eaves. I looked up and saw through the open doorway three men whom I recognized from their dress and their pigtails as belonging to the Lisu tribe. I surmised that it must be a matter of moment that would bring a Lisu some hundred miles through the jungle in the rains to my headquarters. I packed the old man and the buffalo-owner off into a near-by hut with a good tot of rum and a cheroot each, to try, under its soothing influence, to come to some amicable settlement about freehold rights of a spirit in the white tail of a black buffalo.

The three Lisus were then brought before me by a police orderly. They were strong, upright men of Chinese origin, and I noticed that each had in one of his ears a small piece of what looked like pink bone or coral. The Lisus value this ornament very highly, and many a time had I tried in vain to purchase a specimen. But they would not sell. They told me that the bone grows on the leaves of a tree on a certain mountain which is very hard to find. If you are very lucky, they say, and if the moon is in the right quarter you may find the mountain and the tree. Having found it, you must shoot at the topmost leaves with your cross-bow, and maybe a fragment of the pink charm will fall at your feet.

But these three men had matters of more immediate urgency to report; and as I listened I heard unfolded before me the Eastern version of an age-old tragedy. One of their tribe, an old man, had married a young girl from another village, and a few weeks previously had gone with his wife to her parents' home for a visit. It happened to be the time of the gathering in of the paddy harvest, and there were to be the usual feasts customary on such occasions. A week or so later the old man had returned to his own village alone and very sick. He called his friends and relations about him and told them that he had been poisoned by his young bride. As they had been sitting round the fire, drinking the rice-beer from their bamboo cups, he told them, his wife had sidled up behind him and replenished his vessel. She had then invited him to drink with her, and as he drank he knew that he had been poisoned. He had felt the cold chill of it as it passed down his throat. He had left the feast and returned to his own people so that they might know and take revenge. In order that no proof should be lacking, he instructed them to lay his body on an untanned tiger skin, and when he died the very poison that had been used would ooze out of the ends of his fingers and toes. This they had done, and when the old man died they collected the poison in a little bamboo phial. A few days later the girl had appeared at their village, asking what had become of her husband. They had accused her of poisoning him, but this she denied. When ordered to prove her innocence by drinking the liquid which had been collected from her late husband's extremities she—very naturally, I thought—refused. And now the village had sent this delegation to me, and, laying the little bamboo phial on the table, they asked for justice. I opened the phial and was astonished to see that it contained a quantity of quicksilver. My knowledge of poisons was very vague, but I felt that there was something in this strange but not inexplicable story, and that an investigation was indicated. Next morning I set out from Konglu for the scene of the tragedy.

Travelling during the rains is one of the least pleasant experiences of life on the North-east Frontier, and that journey was no exception. With a small escort and a party of Nung porters, I trod a wearisome and slippery way across the hills to the village where the old man had died. The flimsy bamboo bridges across the swift mountain streams were rotten with the rains. In one place the whole road for a distance of some fifty yards had slipped into the valley below. Leeches waved their attenuated, hungry forms from the tips of every blade of grass, an instinctive reaction to the sound of human or animal approach. When I had first come across these objectionable creatures it had been my custom to make an orderly march behind me armed with a bamboo stick on the end of which was a pad of wet salt. It had been his duty to dab every leech that he saw settle on me, but I had long since given up this hopeless battle. I had ceased to bother about them, and they would cling to my stockinged legs till, glutted with blood, they fell off, to be squashed in a gory mess by the feet of the porters behind. They would climb up my stick and feed from the palms of my hands. They did not hurt, however, and I never suffered any harm from them, the only inconvenience being the blood-soaked state of my stockings and boots when my boy removed them at the end of each march.

After ten days' arduous travel I arrived at the village, where I found further corroboration of the tale told me by the three Lisus. The girl had returned to her home, and thither I followed her. News travels fast, even in this sparsely inhabited, difficult country, and I knew that she must already be well aware that I was on her track. I also knew that she would not travel far from her own village. Her area of safety was strictly limited, and I was mildly astonished that she had even been allowed to return alive to her own home. It was late one afternoon when we came in sight of the village, a collection of thatched huts on a spur by the river. It had been a trying day's march, and at one point we had to build a raft in order to cross a stream where the bridge had completely collapsed. I was walking well ahead of my party, as was my custom, when I noticed great red blotches of blood on the path. These were the remains of squashed leeches and were indicative of a party ahead. It was also evident by the freshness of the blood that they were not far off and I quickened my pace. I came upon them very suddenly, three women and a boy, about a quarter of a mile from the village. I stopped to speak to them, making known—not that it was necessary—the mission on which I had come. Then one of them, who had hung back, stepped forward and said that she was Ayaw, the girl whom I sought. I cannot say that I was surprised at this surrender; I had ceased to be surprised at anything east of Suez. But I was surprised at the comeliness of this girl-wife. Her face might not have been exactly such as to launch a thousand ships, but it was of a beauty and charm rarely to be found in these parts. Her long black hair, encircled by the headdress of beads common to Lisu women, hung down in two heavy plaits behind her broad but shapely shoulders. Her features were regular, her complexion fair, and she had an affection of the right eyelid which caused it to droop and flicker in a perpetual and not unattractive wink. The words of an old song began to run through my mind: 'For youth cannot mate with age.' I too was young, and it occurred to me that this case might provoke some heart-stirring perplexities.

I returned with Ayaw to Konglu, and very glad I was to see the little outpost again. Once, *en route,* she had escaped and disappeared in the jungle, but after three days' search she had been retaken, and, much against my will, I had been forced to put her in handcuffs. On arrival at Konglu, I made doubly sure of her security by the addition of leg-irons, and then settled down to the routine of her trial on the charge of murder.

Day after day Ayaw squatted by the side of my table, her chains clanking with every movement, while the witnesses made their depositions and answered my interrogations, but never a word did she speak. She would not plead. Apparently she took no interest in the Proceedings, but she kept her eyes fixed on my face, and as her right eyelid flickered and drooped I felt an uneasiness stirring within me. At first it was pity for her; she was so young and so fair, and, from all accounts, the old man had been a bit of a tartar. I began to feel that my judgment in the case was becoming biassed, that I was acting more in the capacity of counsel for the defence than that of a strictly impartial magistrate. Then my eyes would fall on that little bamboo phial on the table, and I would pull myself together. But at night I would sit by my fire in the little bungalow and think of Ayaw and her youth and her beauty. Women till then had meant very little to me physically, and, being away at school most of my life, I had had little to do with girls when I was a youth. My first bite at the apple had been taken at Mandalay. No Eve had tempted me, but I had been curious to know more about this wonderful experience of which I had heard men talk. It had all been very decently arranged, and I fear that my impressions were that the pastime had been a little over-rated. Nevertheless, youth, beauty, and passion in a woman interested and attracted me. Ayaw possessed the first two in a marked degree, and I had a feeling that the third was there, latent, waiting to be roused. So night after night I sat and dreamed of Ayaw until an overwhelming aching and yearning seized upon my soul, and one night I fell.

It was as if every one in the outpost except myself had expected this to happen. The guards brought Ayaw up to the bungalow and silently withdrew to their own quarters. No questions were asked, no explanations given; it all seemed so natural, as if it had all happened before and would all happen again as the harvest follows the sowing. And most of all did it seem natural to Ayaw as she moved across the little room and seated herself on the floor by the fire. She did not speak, but stretched her hands out to the blaze, the firelight being reflected back in tiny points of red light from her handcuffs and irons. I did not remove these, but sat looking at her for a long while in silence. I then stretched out my hands and took her slender fingers in mine, and we rose to our feet. As I looked down into her eyes the faintest of blushes suffused her high cheek-bones, and she whispered the first word I had heard her speak for many days: '*Duwa*' ('Chief'). Judge and prisoner kissed, and all the man-made ethics and moralities were forgotten in the passionate call of youth to youth. During the long hours of that night, as I lay as surely in the chains of passion as she was in those of iron, Ayaw told me how she had poisoned her husband, how a young Chinese lover from over the border had given her the poison, and how she had put it into the old man's liquor and made him drink to his fair young wife.

It was 'the lark and not the nightingale' which brought me back to my senses the next morning. The case had been closed, but no verdict had yet been given. Being, as I have said, very vague about poisons, I had written to Mandalay to find out whether mercury, taken internally, would cause death. As may be imagined, it was with some anxiety that I awaited the reply to my letter. Nearly two months passed before I received it, and then it was to the effect that mercury was poisonous if certain salts were present in the stomach and that an analysis of the contents of the organ in question would be necessary. As the old man had now been dead over four months this was impossible, and there remained for me the alternative of having the case retried according to local custom. This necessitated calling together a number of chiefs whose tribes were not concerned in the case. These elders were shut up in a special hut with ample supplies of food, tobacco, and rum. Here they stayed for several days discussing and arguing over the tribal customs as they affected the case in question. At length they arrived at a decision, and I summoned them before me to consider their verdict. They found that the charge of murder was not proven, but they found the girl guilty of being unfaithful to her husband and ordered her village to pay a fine of a number of cooking-pots, fowls, etc., to the village of the deceased.

I confirmed the verdict and sentence, and was it my imagination or as Ayaw left the court-room did that right eyelid of hers flicker a little more than usual?

Chapter V

ON TOUR

In 1922 the shadow of the Geddes Axe hung over the Indian Army, and in particular over those officers who had received their commissions during the War. In a vague sort of way I had been cherishing the hope that Army Headquarters had forgotten about me in my little outpost in this out-of-the-way corner of the Empire. But I should have remembered that it was a baboo who, from his desk in a Government office in Simla, had discovered by his calculations the highest mountain in the world, and so in the fullness of time they remembered me. Meanwhile, during the Christmas of that year, I had left my hill-top and descended to the plain of Hkamti Long, where was situated the headquarters of the District. It was usual for the civil and military officers of the District to forgather here at this time of the year, and on this occasion we were expecting two important visitors from Burma, the Commissioner of the Division and the Deputy Inspector General of Military Police. It was here also that I first met that remarkable botanist Kingdon-Ward. I was in the District court-house at the time trying a case which was interesting on account of the variety of the forms of oath required in swearing in the witnesses. There was a Kachin Christian with his Bible, a Kachin Animist who took the oath with his keen-bladed dah held above his head, a Burman who swore by the Buddhist kyansa, and a Burmese woman who also swore on the kyansa but was not allowed to hold it, as she was pregnant. Lastly there was a Chinaman who very emphatically smashed a glass on the court-room floor. It was during these proceedings that I received a note from Kingdon-Ward, and a little later I met him as he strolled casually in from China. He presented a peculiar spectacle as he came into view. He was clad in an old green khaki tunic and slacks and carried a green butterfly-net over his shoulder, while his bearded gaunt face and prominent eyes were shaded by the brim of a felt hat which had long since lost its crown. Every now and then he would stop by the path and examine some plant or fallen seed. An amazing man and an intrepid traveller, he exhibited keen interest in the troupe of Lisu dancers which I had brought from the Ahkyang Valley for the Commissioner's durbar.

Chapter V : On Tour

I took advantage of the presence of the Commissioner in Putao to put forward my application for transfer to the North-east Frontier Service, then in process of formation. Owing to my experience of administration among the tribes, it was kindly received, and with a lighter heart I turned my steps back to Konglu.

Early in January 1923 I started out on the yearly inspection of the eastern part of my territory. This lay in the direction of that snow-capped range of mountains towards which my speculative gaze had so often wandered. It was my duty to collect the taxes, take a rough census of the population, and settle any case which might be pending. I was somewhat surprised at the eagerness with which the Gurkhas had sought selection as escort for this particular tour. True, the weather was ideal for travelling in this kind of country, but I felt that that was not all. A few days' march brought us into the Nung territory, and here an incident enlightened me. The Nungs are a peaceful race, having neither the independent spirit of the Lisus nor, I regret, the cleanliness of the Shans. I had halted one day at one of their villages, and after having carried out my duties as magistrate, tax-gatherer, and benevolent distributor of beads, mirrors, cloth, needles, etc., retired for the night under a mosquito-net in one of the huts. Not long afterwards I was awakened by someone crawling under the net; putting out my hands, I grabbed two heads of thick, bobbed hair and realized that two of the unmarried girls of the village were displaying their hospitality. Firmly, but gently, I declined, but they did not understand, not even when I made them each a present of a mirror. Before turning in again I took a torch and made a round of the sentries. As I passed the hut in which the main body of the escort was sleeping I flashed my torch and looked in. There was a frightened scurry as a number of half-naked brown forms rushed out of the other end of the hut into the night. It was like flushing a covey of partridges. Now I understood, and the more I thought about it the more I sympathized with those young, unmarried Gurkhas. They were far from their native country of Nepal, and leave was expensive and not too frequent. These Nung girls were not immoral, they were unmoral; prostitutes were unknown in this part of the world. Many a time was I stopped in that district by Nung girls who had recognized among my escort the father of a child born since the last tour. There was no bitterness, no regrets, and no recriminations. The Gurkha, looking very like a schoolboy found out in some harmless peccadillo, always acknowledged his paternity, and I, on his behalf, gave the girl flour, rice, cloth, and, perhaps, a little money, all of which would be deducted from the man's pay on his return. It was all very simple, very natural, and, in some ways, rather amusing.

It was shortly after one of these episodes that I received reports of another murder. This time it was a more serious one in that it concerned the son of a Lisu chief who had killed his brother. The details were very meagre, and, as I was due to pass through the Lisu country, I decided to postpone any investigation until I reached that particular village. We continued our journey and reached the banks of the Nmai Hka, entering Lisu country. There was no bridge over this river, flowing swiftly in its deep gorges, and a hazardous crossing was made in a crazy contraption fastened to a pulley which ran on a long fibre rope made fast to trees on either bank. It is the traversing of such natural obstructions that provides the main difficulty of travel in these regions. Bridges are swept away during the rains and have to be replaced during the dry season. This is not a difficult matter, as they are built solely from bamboo and fibre. No nails are used, and I never failed to breathe a sigh of relief when I had successfully negotiated one of these flimsy, high-swung erections which swayed and bent to every footstep.

My main objective, during the last few days, had been a village called Konglanghpu, which was not only the headquarters of the headman of this district, but also the burial place of Reginald Farrer, the naturalist. On arriving near the village I decided to halt for a day or two in order to make an investigation on the spot. The place was in a fever of suppressed excitement because the two brothers involved were the sons of a powerful Lisu chief. There was, of course, no information to be gathered as to the whereabouts of the accused, so I summoned the witnesses before me and proceeded to take evidence. They looked a tough crowd as they sat before me on the floor of the hut. Armed to the teeth with dahs, spears, crossbows, and quiverfuls of poisoned arrows, they formed a semicircle in front of my little camp table, and they gave their evidence fearlessly and, I could not help thinking, truthfully. The facts of the case were simple enough. The scene had been the usual one of the rice-beer feast at the gathering in of the paddy crop. The cause of the quarrel and the subsequent disaster had been a matter of inheritance, a cause of fraternal dissension as old as time. In the heat of the moment the less favoured one had drawn his dah and smitten his brother, and now, apparently, like Cain, was wandering in the wilderness. His brother, before he died, had begged I should be informed that his brother was not to blame. He said the liquor and anger had caused them to lose control, and he prayed that I would be merciful. I had no reason to doubt all this; the Lisus, unlike the Nungs, are an extremely independent and moral race and are too proud to stoop to lying, even to save their own necks.

While I was considering the matter one of my police peons stepped up behind my chair and in a whisper told me that the murderer was one of the dozen or so men before me. 'Which one?' I asked. 'The young one with the charm in his ear, *Duwa.*' I looked at the man indicated, a personable, fearless-looking young man in his early twenties with the usual armoury of primitive but, at close range, very effective weapons. The men in front of me had begun to grow restless and to whisper among themselves; from outside the hut rose the wailing of women. I knew that something must be done and done quickly. 'I shall have to arrest him,' I whispered to my headman. 'But they will fight, *Duwa.* You must promise them that he will not be hanged, and everything may yet be all right.' 'I can't do that,' I said. 'Send me the havildar.' The N.C.O. in charge of my escort came in and saluted. I ordered him to line the escort up outside the hut with fixed bayonets and to be prepared for emergencies. As soon as I heard the reassuring snicks of the bayonets being fixed I rose very slowly, almost casually, from my camp chair and strolled over to the young man. It was a tense moment, and I must admit that I was feeling none too good. He stood up as I approached, and the other tribesmen gathered round, their hands reaching for their dahs. I think that I was very near death then, but I kept my eyes fixed on the lad's face; we were much of an age and height, and I think that it was this that saved me. I carried no arms, and I felt he believed he could trust me to do my utmost for him. No words were exchanged between us. He knew I had discovered his identity. Telling the other men to stand back, he took a step to meet me, and, without any more ado, I slipped a pair of handcuffs over his wrists. It was all over, and the young chief stood there, as if in a trance, gazing down at his manacled hands. He looked like some dumbly protesting captive animal, unable to realize that the freedom of the jungles and the hills was no longer his. I felt keenly sorry for him and patted his shoulder reassuringly, but there was no time to be lost. The wailing of the women and shouts of the men had increased as the other witnesses emerged from the hut unaccompanied by the chief's son. I decided to move downstream and try to reach Konglanghpu before nightfall. The coolies were soon ready, and then, with my arm about the lad's shoulder, I led him out of the hut into the files of the escort. There was a sudden silence as we appeared, but our position seemed somewhat to allay the anger and dismay of the crowd. The order to march was given, and we moved out of the village without incident.

We reached Konglanghpu as dusk fell, and I placed the prisoner under guard in a hut specially erected for that purpose. With him was confined another prisoner, a young Kachin whom I had arrested a day or two previously. His offence was no great matter, merely that of stealing some of my bridge-repairing wire to make bracelets for his lady-love, but wire was at a premium in these parts, 350 miles from a railway, and it was necessary to make an example of him. Here at Konglanghpu the prisoners were to be left under guard, while I continued my tour of the sub-division towards the Chinese border. It was my intention to collect them on my return and take them into Konglu for trial. I was not destined to see one of them again, but that is another story.

2. *Captain Robinson in 1923*

Chapter VI

DEVIL'S DICE

Reginald Farrer's grave at Konglanghpu lies on a ridge overlooking the confluence of the Ahkyang River and the Nmai Hka. It is a simple affair, consisting of a roughly hewn wooden cross, surrounded by a low post-and-rail fence. To the east rises the lofty, snow-capped range of mountains which marks the Chinese frontier and where, shortly before my arrival, he had died a solitary death, deserted by his porters but succoured to the last by his faithful cook. Not very far away is another grave, typical of many that one may pass on those hilly jungle roads. But here a wooden coffin, with a head-piece carved and painted in the semblance of a hawk's head, lies in the open. On it are the rotting blanket and clothes of its occupant, and over all has been erected a little conical shelter of leaves. It is the grave of an old man who should have known better than to expect exotic blooms to thrive in the shade, who drank of a cup and died of an exudation of mercury. The people of this district are kindly and tolerant, and the graves, Christian and Animist, are not disturbed.

On the day I left Konglanghpu for my tour up the Ahkyan Valley I was joined by a Chinese spy from over the border. He did not exactly report his arrival to me, though even that would not have been surprising, but I was made aware of his presence within an hour of his arrival. Clad in the usual blue shirt and trousers, he was a cheerful soul and was of great assistance in helping to distribute loads among the porters at the commencement of each day's march. I had many a long talk with him over the camp fire in the evening, when he would tell me about his master, my opposite number on the other side of the border, and how excellent it would be if a meeting could be arranged. The territory in which I was now travelling had long been claimed by China, and a few years previously many exciting skirmishes had taken place in these hills between the Military Police and the Chinese. The Lisus, as I have said, are of Chinese origin and wear the pig-tail, but I hear that it was a more mercenary motive, that of taxation, that drew the covetous eyes of the local War-lord to this area. For some time there had been little trouble between the two administrations, and I felt that there was nothing to fear from this little Chinaman who was so useful in looking after the baggage. So he went about, assiduously making notes of my doings, and when we met at the end of a long day's march the subject of espionage was tactfully avoided.

Early one February afternoon I entered a village on the Ahkyang which, though I did not know it at the time, was to be the scene of a decision on my part, which was to have a definite bearing on the future. The village was connected to another village on the opposite bank by a bamboo bridge, and I found the inhabitants of both villages in a state of angry excitement. It appeared that there was a bitter dispute over the ownership of a buffalo calf, and things looked serious. Both villages produced a female buffalo, supposed to be the mother of the calf. The difficulty appeared insoluble, until in desperation I decided on a plan. Ordering the two headmen to take their respective mother-buffaloes to their own ends of the bridge, I led the calf by a rope to the centre of the swaying structure. At a given signal from me two of the Gurkhas prodded the two ladies with their bayonets, and as soon as they started to bellow their protests I let the youngster off his lead. The villagers were so amused by the novelty of the proceedings that no further objection was raised by the village whose buffalo had failed to attract the calf.

Returning to my hut, I found a dispute in process between the military and civil members of my party. It was a small matter—as to which of them should have the open-door end of a long, thatched hut which had been allotted to them. Such differences of opinion on their order of precedence were apt to arise between the Gurkhas and the Kachins, and up to this time I had managed to avoid friction by arranging that they should have separate quarters. In this village, however, that had not been possible, and, hearing a commotion, I went out to investigate. I was tired, I had had a long march and a trying day's work at the end of it, and this petty squabbling over the sleeping quarters seemed the last straw. One of my best Kachin assistants, a nice young lad from down country, was arguing vehemently with the Gurkha havildar. Goaded with irritability, I struck him, and as he staggered back I saw on his face a look of mingled anger and pain. It was wrong to have struck him. I had never before laid my hand on anyone under my command, but it was doubly wrong to have struck him before the Gurkhas and the villagers. I returned to my hut, feeling very tired and sick at heart, and sat down in my camp chair. On the little table before me was a bundle of letters, just brought in by a native runner, and a small pile of little brownish cubes of various sizes. These little cubes, perfect in shape, had been found on that morning's march in the sandy content of an excavation by the side of the path. The villagers had told me that they could only be obtained at that one spot, and out of curiosity I had collected a few specimens.

I looked through my mail and found one letter which contained news not unexpected. The Geddes Axe had fallen, and after the completion of my tour I was to return to Mandalay. Sick and tired as I was on that particular evening, this news scarcely had the power to depress me further, and as I sat there alone in the dusk I thought of the look on that Kachin lad's face, and I thought of other things. I began to wonder whether I was really intended for this solitary life. There was my application for the Frontier Service; that would almost certainly go through, and then I should have to spend the remainder of my active days cut off, more or less, from people of my own race. Could I endure it, or was I too young? No white women were allowed to enter Putao, and... there had been that case of Ayaw. There was still time for me to withdraw that application and then I should go down to Mandalay. Mandalay! That name had always sounded sweet in my ears, and never had it sounded more sweet than now, here in my isolation among races whom, although I could admire and respect, I could never love. I thought of the old fort with the moat and bridges; I thought of the golden-mohur trees and the soft tinkling of the little bells on the *htis* of the pagodas, and a great wave of home-sickness surged over me. I took pen and paper and wrote a request to have my application for the Frontier Service cancelled. I would go home—I would go back to Mandalay. I called the runner and, sealing the letter, I dispatched him forthwith on his hundred and fifty mile run back to Konglu. The decision was made, and as I leaned back in my chair, my fingers touched the little cubes on my table. 'Miners call them the Devil's Dice,' I mused to myself, 'and they are supposed to indicate the presence of gold.' But all the gold I wanted was the sight of the golden-mohur trees round the moat at Mandalay after a shower of rain.

Chapter VII

A TOUCH OF MAGIC

It was with a light heart that I left that village the next morning and turned my steps towards that towering, snowy rampart which lay before me. Even a report from Konglanghpu that the chief's son, whom I had left there under guard, had escaped failed to worry me overmuch. It was a nuisance, but out here I could do nothing about it. Investigation would have to wait till my return there.

Three days' march brought us to our objective, and we halted in a village at the foot of the pass. The villagers were very friendly, and on the afternoon of our arrival I improvised some sports in which both the Gurkhas and the Lisus participated. The prizes were the usual lengths of cloth, pipes, mirrors, beads, and needles which I carried with me as presents for the natives. Owing to the difficulty of finding any considerable stretch of level ground in these parts, the flat races had to be run along the narrow road cut in the hillside. Everything went well until the ladies' race. There was room enough on the path for two normal persons to pass or overtake. Unfortunately, in this race the lead was taken at the start by a slow but over-developed matron. Her naked breasts, hanging down to her waist, swayed so violently and effectively from side to side as she ran, that none of the younger and more fleet-footed of the competitors was able to pass without the risk of receiving one of them in her face.

In the evening we sat round a big log fire in the centre of one of the huts while some of the Lisus, in two opposed lines, performed their tribal dances. They swayed to music provided by species of bamboo Jew's-harps and one-stringed fiddles, the strings of the fiddles and bows being made from human hair. In order to provide a little variety to the entertainment, I performed a simple conjuring trick. Having concealed three matches in the hem of my handkerchief, I showed the apparently empty piece of linen to the assembled Lisus and asked one of them to place a match in it. Folding up the handkerchief, I allowed one of the men to feel and break what he thought must be the match which had just been placed therein. I then turned to a small brass figure of Buddha which I always carried about with me and which was standing on my camp table. Bowing to this three times, I invoked a blessing on my magic and, opening the handkerchief, displayed the match unbroken. It was a simple trick but seemed miraculous to my audience. I was able to repeat the trick twice more, and they were amazed.

While they were discussing this wonderful phenomenon, a youthful Nung porter rose from the circle and asked me whether I could perform the fire-magic. On my inquiring the nature of this magic he stretched forth his arm and thrust his hand into the midst of the blazing log fire. For what seemed an incredible time he played with the white-hot embers in the centre of the flaming mass. Then, drawing out a portion of the burning wood, he proceeded to draw it all over his naked body, leaving streaks of black, grey, and white ash as the white-hot brand cooled against his skin. It was an astonishing spectacle, but seemed to cause no surprise among the other onlookers. I could not bear my hand within two feet of the fire, the heat was so fierce. The most striking thing about this display was that the performer was a simple Nung porter, of no importance in his tribe or village, and the act was performed without any thought of financial gain. I have seen many apparently miraculous feats performed by wandering conjurors in India, but the peculiar circumstances of this present manifestation of abnormal power by a simple Nung coolie left no doubt in my mind as to its genuineness.

Early the next morning I commenced the climb to the summit of this thirteen-thousand-foot pass where I hoped to find a small cairn of stones. This marked the frontier between Burma and China, and it was my duty to see that no Chinese War-lord had been rude enough to push it over with his foot. Thus are the boundaries of Empire kept inviolate!

The climb was a long and difficult one, but the scenery was magnificent. The snow-line was reached at about eight thousand feet, and here the big scarlet ball-like clusters of rhododendron blossoms made vivid splashes of colour as they peeped through the snow-covered foliage of the trees, or lay, like huge drops of blood, on the white mantle of the earth. My Kachin servant, who, with my orderly and the tame spy, accompanied me, was much impressed. He had never been among the snow before, and I found him filling a piece of bamboo with the strange stuff so that he might take it back to show his wife. I think that he suspected me of some hidden trickery when, on returning to camp that evening, he found nothing but water.

We reached the summit before noon and found the cairn of stones, neat and symmetrical, but, strange to say, without any covering of snow. By the side of it stood the figure of a young man, a Chinaman, clothed, if not sumptuously, at any rate in a manner which showed him to be of a class superior to the local inhabitants of those parts. My little spy ran forward to greet him, and I very soon learned that he was the son of my opposite number and was the bearer of an invitation from his father for me to visit him. I thought that it would have been more polite of the old gentleman to have met me personally, but I was feeling the strain of the long climb, and a midday rest and hospitality were very welcome.

The Chinese magistrate, who evidently knew all about my movements, had taken up his temporary quarters in an old disused fort, a little way down the mountain-side. He came out to greet me, explaining with profuse apologies that an attack of rheumatism had prevented him from having the honour of meeting me at the frontier. He looked a dissolute old man, but appeared to travel with a considerable degree of comfort. The son was a fine-looking young man and was evidently the apple of his father's eye. He waited on us during the meal and then withdrew, appearing a little later with two small glasses and an earthenware pot, the mouth of which was covered with parchment or skin. The old man broached the vessel and filled the two glasses with a colourless liquid. But whatever rice-spirit may lack in colour, it makes up in smell and fire. It always reminded me of very strong, rank gin which has been kept in a stale beer-bottle. However, I forced myself to drink the vile stuff, and then followed an old Chinese custom. He threw back his wicked old head, the wizened throat rippled convulsively, and he placed the empty glass upside-down on the table. 'It is finished,' he said, and I emptied my own glass and turned it on the table. They were quickly refilled by the son, but now it was my turn to set the pace. According to the rules of the game, I could take as long as I liked, within reason, over my drink, but, as soon as I had finished and up-ended the glass, my friend opposite would have to drain his. The glasses would then be again replenished, and so the game would go on until one or the other of us slid gently under the table. But I did not feel like playing that day; I had a long and arduous descent to my camp, and I had to have my wits about me. Consequently I lingered over my round and began to exchange small-talk with my host. Was all well in China? Yes, things were well enough except that he missed the flesh-pots of the cities. Now, he went on, if we had been in Yunnan-fu he could have given me a feast and entertainment worthy of such an occasion. He went on to expatiate on the delights of newly born white mice dipped in syrup: 'You take one by the tail, you see, and dip him in the syrup. You then lift him up and...' Closing his eyes, he threw back his head and gulped. 'And very nice, too,' I said politely. The glasses were refilled. 'And how are things in the Ahkyang?' he asked. I explained that all was well and thanked him for the assistance I had received from the little Chinaman who had joined me at Konglanghpu. His bleary old eyes smiled benignly from behind his spectacles. 'No matter, no matter,' he croaked. 'But I am glad to hear that all is well in the Ahkyang. You see, sir, my son has, much against my will, taken to himself a wife from among the Lisus.' 'I'm sure that I wish them happiness,' I said, raising my glass and turning round to where the young man was seated, and there, on the mat beside him, was... Ayaw. But what a difference. Gone were the rough clothing and beads of the Lisu girl, and in their place she wore the neat black coat and pyjamas of a Chinese maiden. I confess that my heart missed a beat as I gazed at that oval face beneath the neatly oiled and coiffured hair. She said nothing, but I fancied that I detected the faintest of pink in her ivory-coloured cheeks. As I emptied my glass she raised her eyes to mine and that cursed—no, let me be fair—that bewitching right eyelid seemed to flicker with grave amusement. I turned back to the old sinner opposite me. 'It is finished,' I said, laying down my glass. Yes,' he agreed slowly, 'it is finished.'

Very soon afterwards I made an excuse to get away. I fear that my host thought me rather a poor sport as I declined to stay and play with him at his abominable game. But as I hastened through the snow down to my camp I could not help wondering whether he knew as much about Ayaw as I did, and whether, perhaps, one day he might not drain his glass and say 'It is finished' for the last time as he felt something cold and chilly sliding down his wizened old throat.

Chapter VIII

THE FIVE VIRGINS

Leaving the Ahkyang proper, I continued my tour in a more northerly direction up the Latagaw Valley. Nothing untoward occurred to mar the even trend of the days' marches. My mind was occupied with thoughts of the decision I had recently taken. Eight years' service in the Indian Army does not provide one with the type of training that is likely to be of use in any other sphere, but I was optimistic, with that vague, daydreaming optimism common to the young and those inexperienced in the hard ways of business life.

It was in such a daydream that one morning I rounded the shoulder of an immense spur and, halting for a moment to admire the view, saw two tiny dots by the river far below me in the valley. Out of curiosity I focused my field-glasses on them and by their clothes made them out to be two Chinamen. It was not unusual to meet an occasional Chinese trader selling his sheep or rock-salt among the villages, but these men did not seem to fit into that category. For one thing, they were far removed from the inter-village tracks to which any respectable trader would keep; and for another, I was kept well informed of the movements of most foreigners in my subdivision, and I could not place these men at all. I accordingly detailed a couple of the local police to descend into the valley, find out what the men were doing there, and, if it were anything out of the ordinary, bring them in to me at the next village.

On arriving at the village, which was close to the frontier and near the source of the Latagaw, I took up my quarters in a hut and went through the usual business of settling cases and collecting taxes. It was late in the evening before I had finished, and when my orderly reported that two Chinamen were outside I had them brought before me. They were nothing exceptional in appearance, but their manners and turn of speech made me feel that they were trying to hide something. They were traders, were they? Then where were their trade goods—their sheep or their salt? They had sold them, had they? Then where was the money they had received? A few rupees were located in a knot in one of the men's waist-cloths. I was tired and wanted my evening meal. This prevarication was getting on my nerves. 'Do you think I'm a fool?' I roared. 'What were you doing down in that river-bed?' There is nothing like an empty stomach to form a good foundation for genuine British wrath. The men stepped back a pace or two, and then, undoing a little cloth bag, poured out on to my camp table nugget upon nugget of shining gold. They formed a rich little collection as they lay there on the green canvas. Some appeared to be of pure gold, about the size of beans, others were lumps of white quartz interspersed with veins of gold. I turned them over in my fingers. So the Devil's Dice had not lied after all—at least, not from the material interpretation of their significance.

A few further inquiries elicited the information that it was the custom of these two men to visit this area each year as soon as the passes were open. Did they not know that it was illegal to prospect without a licence? No, they did not know. They were very sorry. I selected a few samples of the nuggets and quartz and, after long argument and the use of a very peculiar pair of scales, paid over a number of silver rupees. I then dismissed the men, telling them that if they were seen in this valley again without permission my successor might not be so lenient. Then, marking the position on my map, I put the nuggets away in a little box with the Devil's Dice, and turned to my meal. Gold! Yes, I knew that there was gold up here in the north of Burma. I had admired the pure golden, twisted bracelets worn by the Shan women in the Hkamti plain. There had been a company which had dredged for gold in the Irrawaddy above Myitkyina. I was no geologist, but that evening I allowed my fancy full play, quite forgetting the fact that I was some five hundred miles from a railway and that the going in between was some of the worst imaginable. I had golden dreams that night, dreams of golden nuggets hanging from golden-mohur trees, and when I awoke the next morning it was to see an apparently golden Buddha gazing down at me from my table with his inscrutable eyes.

The next morning we turned westward, climbing the 9,000-foot Ka-ang Pass over an intervening ridge and dropping from its snow-covered summit into a valley running parallel to the Latagaw. Two or three days' march down this valley would eventually lead us back to Konglanghpu, but I decided to make a halt at a village close to the junction of the valley with that of the Ahkyang. This was the village to which belonged my second prisoner, the lad who had stolen the wire to make bracelets for his girl friend. Apparently he was still safe under guard at Konglanghpu and had not made his escape with the son of the chief. It seemed to me that it would save a lot of time and trouble if I settled his case in his own village and before his own tribe, and a messenger was accordingly sent on ahead with the necessary instructions.

The case was simple, but the question of punishment was more difficult. The crime in itself was not serious, but there were circumstances which rendered it necessary to make an example of the lad. In Burma the intrinsic value of the wire stolen would have been trifling, but it had to be remembered that this particular wire had been brought some three or four hundred miles up-country by mule and coolie and that its value had increased in proportion. I asked the lad if he would prefer a term of imprisonment at Konglu or a flogging, and I was not surprised when, without hesitation, he accepted the latter. Had he ever witnessed a real Army flogging he might have chosen differently, but his simple trust in the innate kind-heartedness of his subdivisional officer was not misplaced.

The villagers were assembled, and a tripod of poles erected in front of my hut. The escort was formed up with bayonets fixed—not that I expected any trouble, but it was always well to be prepared, and, anyway, it made the proceedings more impressive. The prisoner was stripped to the waist and tied by his wrists to the poles. I then made a short speech to the villagers, explaining the great gravity of the offence and the inconvenience to which it had put me. At a sign from me the Gurkha N.C.O. in charge of the escort laid on twelve of the best. It touched the lad up considerably, but he never murmured. A quarter of an hour later he was sitting before the fire in my hut, a free man without malice, beseeching me that he might be taken on as one of my policemen. I liked the lad: I liked the way in which he had chosen and taken his beating, and I consented. Then, having filled his belly with rice and washed it down with rum, he told me of the escape of the chief's son, and, as I listened and heard of the lad's part in the affair I knew that my confidence in his character had not been mistaken.

The two prisoners had been confined, as I have already stated, in a hut built specially for that purpose at Konglanghpu. Rising from the centre of the floor of this hut was a wooden cage, complete with door and padlock. On the floor of the hut around this cage slept those members of the guard who were not on duty. The prisoners were handcuffed, the key being in the charge of the guard commander, and only left the cage for the purposes of nature. The N.C.O. had reported to me that it was on one of these excursions to the edge of the jungle that the young chief had snapped open his handcuffs and disappeared into the undergrowth before the sentry had a chance to do anything about it. The handcuffs were alleged to be faulty, and altogether it was a likely enough story and would probably have passed muster had it not been for this cheerful wire-stealing young

Lothario who was seated before me, wriggling his back while a friend applied soothing lotion to the weals left by the strokes of the cane bamboo.

It appeared that, after my departure from Konglanghpu, members of the young chief's tribe began to drift into the village. There were never enough to excite suspicion, but there were always some there to exchange a few words with the prisoner, words unintelligible to the Gurkhas, as they went to and from the jungle verge. In such manner were the plans for the escape made. The next step in the plan was the arrival one fine morning of five beautiful hill-girls specially selected from the young man's tribe for their freshness and allure. It must be remembered that the Lisus, unlike the Nungs, are a very moral race, but the stakes in the present case—the life of their beloved chief—were such that they were prepared to sacrifice even this reputation in order to secure his freedom. They knew the Gurkhas of old, and they knew what bait to use. I can well imagine how the eyes of those five young reprobates glistened when they beheld this bevy of comeliness. The four who were not on duty were not long in getting acquainted and very soon had adjourned to a hut a little way off. The fifth Gurkha, the sentry, resisted the advances of the fifth virgin for what he considered, no doubt, to be quite a considerable time—probably about two minutes—and then followed his companions.

No sooner had he disappeared than the young chief became an active, quick-witted entity. Stretching his manacled wrists above his head, he drew down between the top bars of his cage a bamboo rod which happened to be lying there. Taking this in his hands, he thrust it between the side bars and with it, hooked up the keys of the guard commander which were lying against the wall near his pillow. He drew the bunch carefully into the cage and unlocked his handcuffs. It was then that he offered to undo the handcuffs of the other prisoner, but the lad refused. He had done no very great crime, he had said, and was prepared to take what was coming to him. The young chief had then pushed the bunch of keys back to their original position and replaced the bamboo rod on the top of the cage. He then replaced his handcuffs, fastening them lightly with a strip of bamboo, and pulled the long sleeves of this coat over all. Everything was now ready, and he called loudly for the sentry. The latter was, no doubt, very annoyed at being thus disturbed, but he came out eventually and took the prisoner to the edge of the jungle; the rest was easy. With a quick jerk of his wrists, he had snapped the bamboo fastening, and the handcuffs had fallen away. Before the sentry, whose mind was on other things, had time to do anything the young chief had been swallowed up in the jungle.

Chapter VIII : The Five Virgins

I sat staring into the fire for a long time after the lad had finished his tale. It had been clever, very clever, and had revealed a strategy and psychological knowledge rare among hill-tribes such as these. I knew that it would be useless to go after the man now; he would be far away and well hidden by this time. And as for the guard, what should I do with them? I thought of Ayaw and that night at Konglu when physical passion had betrayed my sense of duty. Who was I to cast a stone? I sighed a little wearily, stretched my legs, and went to bed.

Chapter IX

'COME YOU BACK TO MANDALAY'

My tour of the Ahkyang was now complete, and nothing remained for me but to return to Konglu and hand over to my successor. The night before I left there was a touching little ceremony on a small level space which had been cut out of the hillside about fifty yards below my hut. Here were gathered Gurkhas, Lisus, Kachins, Nungs, and Marus, who presented me with a loyal address from my people at Konglu. It was written by my Indian clerk, and I transcribe it in full below:

> To Captain H. R. Robinson
> Sir,
> We the people of Konglu have assembled here this evening to express our heartfelt sorrow at the impending departure of our kind-hearted commanding & civil officer.
> To brilliant qualities of head you combine equally noble qualities of heart. Your sympathy, your ready help, your never-failing courtesy, your easy accessibility in spite of the pressing demands on your valuable time, your loving and amiable disposition will always remain a theme of genuine praise amongst us.
> It is at the thought of separation that we realize more than ever what a treasure inestimable you have been to us. In memory of your departure we wish to open a Reading & Recreation Club on your name with your kind permission and encouragement, naming 'Robinson Reading & Recreation Club.'
> In conclusion we wish you a very pleasant journey and safe voyage every happiness & joy in your dear own country sweet home.
> We heartily welcome Captain Hanna and humbly request him to be the patron of the club.
> We are,
> *Beloved Sirs,*
> Your loyal & loving people of Konglu

As regards the 'Reading and Recreation Room,' which they desired to name after me, there was not and, if I knew anything about Konglu, never would be any such place. But they had done their best by digging out this patch of earth and erecting an old badminton net. On a rickety table near by were one or two old copies of *The Sketch* and *La Vie Parisienne*. What did it matter that no one could read them and that, if they should ever play badminton, a mis-hit would send the shuttlecock sailing a thousand or so feet on to the jungles below? I must confess that at that moment even thought of Mandalay failed wholly to soothe the little pang of regret that I felt at parting from these, my 'loyal and loving people', who had always trusted and, I hope, respected me. I still have that letter, and one day maybe, when St Peter is about to slam the golden gates in my face, I may find it useful.

It was towards the end of March that I left Konglu. Never again, I thought, would I hold such a position of responsibility and have the fate of so many people in my hands. I was going back to a life and a civilization where men were judged by more complicated standards than primitive instinct and natural tolerance. Yes, I valued more highly the opinion of these Kachins, Lisus, and Nungs than any favourable report on my work which might have emanated from the Commissioner's office at Maymyo.

Day after day, mile after mile, I followed that long, winding hill-road down the right bank of the Mali Hka. And gradually, imperceptibly as a dream merges into the consciousness of waking thoughts, the friendly memories of my life in that little frontier outpost were swallowed up in the vivid anticipation of my return to Mandalay. During the long journey to Myitkyina I had been turning over in my mind plans for the future. There was due to my gratuity, six months' leave on full pay, and a free passage to England. It was eight years since I had been home; it would be springtime, and the primroses and violets would be out in the Surrey woods. That was a pleasant thought. Much as I loved the jungle, I had become a little oppressed by the profusion and abnormality of its butterflies and orchids. The orchids especially, unhealthy in their beauty and texture, parasites of the jungle, were too vividly reminiscent of the painted ladies of Kariah Lane and Grant Road. It would be refreshing to walk again in an English garden and see the daisies growing on an English lawn. Then, when the summer was over, I would return to Burma, where I would be content to spend the rest of my days among the people whom I loved so well. With such thoughts in my mind, I boarded the train at Myitkyina and, one morning in early April, arrived in Mandalay.

Chapter X

THE INNER ROOM

The formalities in connexion with my retirement from the Indian Army did not take long to complete, and a passage had been reserved for me on a ship sailing for England at the beginning of May. Meanwhile I gave myself up whole-heartedly to the fascination of this former capital of the Burmese kings. I had conceived a great affection for Mandalay ever since the day when I had first driven through the South Gate of the Fort, a newly commissioned subaltern in the newest of Sam Browne belts. In those days most of my activities had been confined to the Fort, a mile-square enclosure containing the infantry lines, mess, club, polo ground, and the old and rather tawdry palace. I had not had much to do with the people, but, nevertheless, it must have been then that the first seeds of enchantment were planted in my soul. It was only now, as I drove my car round the moat or through the city down to the banks of the Irrawaddy, that I realized how deeply rooted were the bonds that held me, but—I was a willing slave. The happy-go-lucky Burmese in their gay clothes, the Buddhist priests in their yellow robes, the pagoda-studded Mandalay Hill, the broad Irrawaddy with its paddle-steamers and sampans, the tinkling of the little bells on the pagoda *htis*—these were a source of sheer delight and serene contentment to me. Yes, it would be pleasant to see England again, but this, all this, was home to me, and I faced the thought of parting in the sure knowledge that I would return.

One evening, towards the end of April, I was sitting in the Upper Burma Club discussing my plans with two friends, whom I will call the Poet and the Padre. As the conversation lagged and there seemed to be nothing to do, the Poet suggested that we should go down to the bazaar and have something to eat at a Chinese restaurant. A visit to the Mandalay bazaar would have appealed to me at any time, but at night it possessed a double fascination. We accordingly got in our cars and drove down to an eating-house in a main thoroughfare not far from the Clock Tower.

There were a few Chinese customers on the ground floor, so we went up a rickety flight of stairs to an upper room which had a balcony overlooking the street. A table and chairs were placed out on this balcony, and there we sat down to do our best with chop-sticks and noodles. But,

Chapter X : The Inner Room

as usual, it was the people passing and repassing in the street below who held my attention. This Eastern city at night, the various nationalities, the babel of tongues, the quaint shop signs, the lighted streets, and the dark, very dark, alleys, filled me with a dreamy intoxication—I yearned to steep myself in it all and find out what was going on up those dark alleys and what thoughts were passing behind those brown faces. I came to myself with a start, as if awakened from a dream, when the Padre said that it was time to be getting back.

As we crossed the upper room to the head of the stairs I noticed that one corner of the room had been partitioned off so as to make, as it were, an inner room about seven feet square. A dim light shone through little shutters in the two exposed walls, and I was able to discern the movement of a punkah within. My curiosity was instantly roused. Telling my friends that I would join them in a minute, I moved quietly towards the inner room and, finding a sliding door, opened it gently. I found myself gazing into the eyes of a Chinaman. The whole of the floor of this little chamber was raised some eighteen inches above the ground, and he was lying on his left side, his head resting on a little wooden stand on which was a small pillow. Fastened to the big toe of his right foot was a cord which ran through a pulley on the wall and thence to the punkah, but what held my attention most was a tray on the floor by his side, and a long, curious bamboo pipe which he held in his hand. 'What are you doing?' I asked in a whisper. Why I whispered I don't know, but I do know that the question was superfluous. Although I had never seen it before, I knew that this man was an opium-smoker. I felt a thrill of excitement pass through me as he confirmed my conviction. I slipped out of the room and, running to the balcony, called down to my waiting friends that I would meet them at the Club later. I heard them drive off and went back to the room.

Seating myself cross-legged in the corner, I closed the door after me and turned again to the tray. On it was a little oil-lamp covered with a glass shade with a hole in the top, rather like an inverted flower-pot, a pair of scissors, evidently used for trimming the wick, and a scraper of some sort, probably used in cleaning the pipe. The pipe was unlike any that I had ever seen. It was made of bamboo and was about eighteen inches long. About four inches from one end protruded the bowl, a circular affair, in the centre of which was a small depression pierced by a tiny hole. As I watched the Chinaman took a long needle, like a thin knitting-needle, from the tray and dipped the end in a miniature wooden wine-glass containing some brown viscous stuff which I knew must be the opium. Taking some of the opium on the end of the needle, he held it over the little lamp, and it began to bubble. He dipped the end again in the cup and repeated the cooking process over the hole in the lamp, deftly twirling the needle so that the opium should not drop off. He then began to fashion a pellet of opium on the end of his needle by rolling it to the required shape on the smooth outer surface of the bowl. When he had made the pill to his liking he held the bowl for a second or two over the lamp, presumably to warm it, and then jabbed his needle firmly into the tiny hole in the centre of the little depression. He then carefully withdrew the needle, but the little pill remained stuck. Then, taking the large mouthpiece of the pipe between his lips, he held the bowl with the pill over the lamp. The opium began to bubble and gurgle, and as he drew the smoke in with one long, continuous breath (or perhaps I should say swallowed it) the little pellet became smaller and smaller until it finally disappeared.

I sat watching the rhythmic working of his Adam's apple with keen interest. Now, I thought, is the time when he should close his eyes and pass into a state of ephemeral bliss. But such was not the case; he picked up a tiny, handleless cup and took a sip of China tea. 'That was good,' he said, gazing at me as if I were an abstract vision from another world. 'May I have a smoke?' I asked. 'No,' he replied. 'It is too dangerous here. It you really want to smoke you must go to Ba Ohn.' 'And who is Ba Ohn?' I inquired. Vouchsafing no further explanation, he rose from the platform and slid back the door. I followed him into the outer room and down the rickety flight of stairs to the restaurant below. Crossing the road, he led the way up one of those dark alleys which had excited my imagination as I had sat with the Padre and the Poet on the balcony. They were forgotten now, and forgotten, too, was any code which might have anchored me to my own kin. I was in a fever of excitement. Up and up this dark canyon we went until my guide stopped before a house on the right-hand side, above the door of which a small balcony was revealed in the moonlight. He called softly the name of Ba Ohn. A few seconds' pause, and a voice within answered, inquiring our business. After a brief exchange of explanations the door was opened, and I was led up another flight of very rickety stairs to a room the sight of which made me halt in amazement.

Chapter XI

OPIUM

Facing me was a long wall, and from this wall, about eighteen inches from the ground, projected a platform something over six feet in width. Along this platform were pairs of opium-smokers, Chinese and Burmese mostly, each pair facing inward towards a little lamp and tray such as I had seen in the inner room across the way. There was a faint, a very faint, murmur of conversation, such as one might hear from a child talking in his sleep. Above the glimmer of the tiny lamps and the murmur of the dream-like voices there rose the heavy, soothing smell of the opium. No one took any notice of me... except one man—a mere boy he seemed to be—who now stood bowing before me in blue *engyi* (coat) and multi-coloured *lungyi* (skirt). His hair was long, in the old Burmese tradition, and was held in place by a silken *gaungbaung*. But it was his face, and especially his eyes, that drew my attention. Mongolian in outline, his face was a deathly white, the scarlet of his perfectly shaped lips and the dark, flashing brilliance of his eyes standing out in startling contrast to the ivory pallor of this face. He motioned me to an empty place on the long platform and took his position on the opposite side of the little tray. With deft fingers he commenced to make the opium pill, and I observed the remarkable transparent whiteness of his thin, attractive hands. So this was Maung Ba Ohn. Occasionally during my life I had met men upon whom it was good to look. At school there had been boys whose faces had been a source of perpetual disquiet to me, but never had I met a man whose fascination could compare with that of Ba Ohn. Nevertheless, it was the fascination of the orchid, the fascination of the painted lady, the fascination of something too good to be true.

'You would like to smoke, *thakin*?' Ba Ohn said, in good English. 'Yes,' I replied, my eyes still fixed on those delicate hands. Having prepared the pill, he took the long pipe by the short end and handed the mouthpiece over to me; I took it between my lips and inhaled as one would from a cigarette. The result was disastrous: I coughed and spluttered. Maung Ba Ohn encouraged me to persevere. The next pill was his by usage, and I watched, fascinated, as he inhaled the smoke in one long, effortless intake. We had the usual appurtenances on our tray:

the wicker basket with the tea-pot and the two tiny cups. My next effort was a little more successful, and I managed to take in the whole pill. However, there was something in this business, I thought, that was not according to precedent; surely after smoking opium I should go off into delectable dreams of ineffable bliss. All I felt, apart from the rather fuggy and homely smell of the drug, was a serenity of mind and a disinclination to trouble myself about any matters except the immediate necessity of preparing the next pill. I did not feel sleepy, but the fact that the Padre and the Poet were probably waiting for me at the Club faded into sheer insignificance. The fact of the matter was that I was perfectly content—which is not a good state for any man to be in.

The hours passed, the little wooden goblet was replenished, and I lay there on my right side, my head on a miniature pillow, while Ba Ohn's white transparent hands fashioned pill after pill. We did not talk much, but every time he handed to me the long bamboo pipe his brilliant eyes seemed to speak to me as eloquently as the song of Circe, inviting me to partake of joys as yet undreamed of. Those eyes and those hands! Those delicate feet peeping out beneath the fringe of the silken lungyi! Those gaily coloured clothes, the lungyi and the engyi, that covered a body as emaciated as that of the Blessed Buddha in his time of fasting! Here was the incarnate spirit of Opium. Those eyes, so alluring, had something behind them, a look that knew but ignored fear, a soul haunted by the thoughts of the future. And yet, to me then, he was beauty incarnate.

It was in the early hours of the morning that I bethought myself of my bed. I had smoked I don't know how many pills and had felt none the worse for them until I went into the open air, when I was violently sick. Maung Ba Ohn patted me gently on the shoulder and told me that everything would be all right. 'And when shall I see the *thakin* again?' he asked in his quiet voice. 'Oh, I'm going to England in a week or so,' I said 'But I'll look in again before I go.' He smiled at me, that tantalizing smile of lips and eyes, and said, 'The *thakin* will surely return. I shall always be here to attend on him.' He disappeared into the shadows of that dark alley, and I was left to find my way back to my car. It had been a very pleasant evening. Bed was indicated. I climbed into my car and drove off. As I passed along the main street leading to the road that runs along the South Moat of the Fort I began to feel very sleepy. I thought that it might be better, for safety's sake, to draw up at the side of the road and take a few minutes' nap. I pulled the car up outside a well-known English store and settled down for a short sleep. When I awoke it was broad daylight. There was a large crowd gathered round the car, the headlights of which were on, while a policeman kept them from disturbing me; but the butterfly spirit, which the Burmese believe leaves the body during sleep, had returned, and I drove on my way thrilled, but a little disappointed, with my first taste of opium.

Chapter XII

THE DREAM

Two nights later my car slid silently to a standstill outside the Chinese eating-house, and I slipped across the road into the blackness of the little alley. It was instinct, rather than premeditation, which prompted this cautious method of approach. As I made my way through the darkness a small figure rose, apparently from under my feet, and took me by the hand. It was an Indian boy who had been seated in the shadows and who had evidently been expecting me. In silence he led me to the foot of the staircase, up which he called softly to announce my arrival. I climbed the stairs and entered the room.

The air was heavy with the fumes from half a dozen pipes; the little oil-lamps lit up the faces of the smokers, but there was no sign of curiosity in those eyes as I made my way to where Ba Ohn was lying, smoking alone. I lay down opposite him, on the other side of the tray, and took the pipe he offered me. I was becoming a little more experienced, and as I drank down the smoke in one long, continuous intake a sense of peace and well-being seemed to pervade my whole body and smooth out the mental wrinkles behind my eyes. As Ba Ohn manipulated the next pill for his own smoke I relaxed and considered. The effects of this opium-smoking were very pleasant, but so different from anything I had expected. Where were those dreams of which I had read? I felt somehow that I had been cheated of something, that my curiosity had not received its full reward. I did not even feel sleepy but the physical feeling of languor was certainly pleasant. Perhaps I had not smoked enough? Perhaps... perhaps the dreams would come later.

'So you have come back, *thakin*,' said a low voice from the other side of the tray. I looked up. Ba Ohn had removed the bowl of the pipe and was engaged in removing the opium residue from the inside with the hooked metal scraper. 'Yes,' I replied. 'Were you expecting me?' He smiled in quiet amusement as he replaced the bowl and dipped the needle into the opium cup, preparatory to making the next pill. 'Oh, yes,' he said, 'I knew that you would return—if not to-night, then to-morrow night. And when do you leave for England, *thakin*?' I looked at him, but his dark eyes were veiled by his long lashes, and, except for a slight twitching at the corners of his mobile mouth, there was no expression on his pale face. As it happened, I had cancelled my passage on the previous day and rented a little bungalow in the civil line, south of the Fort. The reason for this sudden change in my plans had been a strong desire to postpone for a time this temporary parting from a city and people to whom I had only so recently been re-united.

'I am not going back just yet,' I said. 'I have taken a house and will bide awhile in Mandalay.' 'Then we shall meet again, *thakin;* beyond doubt we shall meet again.' The words came in a soft, almost caressing whisper, and as I looked at his strangely beautiful face the call of the East was strong within me, and I felt that it would be pleasant, and perhaps interesting, to probe some of its mysteries with such a one to guide me.

It was past midnight when I rose to leave. Any misgivings which I may have had regarding the advisability of postponing my departure for England had been evaporated by the opium. In order to avoid any repetition of my previous sickness on entering the outer air, I had been given and had swallowed one of the prepared pills. The drive back through the warm night was very pleasant, and I managed to reach my house and my bed before sleep overtook me.

It was on that night that I first dreamed that strange dream which troubled me for many weeks. My bed was always placed at night on the open veranda above the porch of the bungalow. Across the road, in this quiet outskirt of the city, was a Buddhist monastery, and often as I lay in bed under the stars I would listen to the sweet tinkling of the little bells on the *hti* of the pagoda and, perhaps, the monotonous intoning of some wakeful and devout *hpongyi*.

But on this night, the night of my dream, things were different. The bells lilted in the night breeze, the *hpongyis* chanted, but I lay there on my bed, my eyes turned up to star-dusted sky, unable to move. I was conscious in an abstract way of the bells and the monks, conscious of the stars in the sky, and acutely conscious of a delicious feeling of languor and limpness in every muscle of my body. No doubt I could have moved if I had so desired, but the mental effort would have been so great that any attempt was unthinkable. Thus it was that I slept and dreamed.

I dreamed that I was travelling through a vast, unknown jungle. I was on a pilgrimage to some ancient and forgotten temple. The jungle and the path were not familiar to me, but for some unaccountable reason I thought that it must be Malaya or Indo-China. As I neared the ancient temple I was met by a beautiful brown-skinned girl, the daughter of the old priest whom I had travelled so far to see. There was something that I was to receive from this old man, something very precious. The girl led me through the crumbling gates of the old city to the stone cell in which she and her father lived. As I entered the open door I saw the old priest lying apparently asleep on a couch. But he was not asleep—he was dead. He had died, the girl explained, about two days previously, but he had known of my search and what it was for which I was searching. It was the key to the mystery of life, the final answer to the eternal 'Why?'. He had written the secret on a slip of parchment which the girl was to remove from his dead hand and give to me on my arrival. I took the slip from the girl's hand and read. Of course, of course, why had man never thought of that before? Now I knew, but...

When I woke next morning I had completely forgotten. Every detail of the dream was clear to me except the actual words which I had read on the parchment.

For three or four weeks this dream came back to me. It only occurred on those nights when I had been down to the opium-den, and as this was now about three times a week, I began to grow more and more anxious to solve the mystery. I knew, through constant repetition, every detail of the dream except the secret itself. It was maddening.

It was one night in June, as I drove back from a rendezvous with Ba Ohn, that I decided to make a supreme effort. I felt that if I could wake myself before the memory of the words had faded I could make a note of them before I fell asleep again. The trouble was to rouse myself sufficiently from my stupor to do the writing. However, when I lay down that night I placed a pencil and pad on a low table close to my bed. The pleasant languor began to permeate my body until, very soon, I felt that I was no longer bound by any ties of the flesh. Then the dream began to form before my eyes: the jungle, the girl, the temple, the cell, the dead man, the parchment. I read, I woke, and, with a superhuman effort of will-power, I forced my opium-soaked body to turn until my hand found the pencil and pad, and then, by the light of the moon, I wrote it down. My object achieved, I fell back and knew no more until I awoke in the morning. The dream was still vivid in my mind up to the point of the reading of the script, and it was a minute or two before I remembered the pad which I had placed by my bed the night before. Suddenly it all came back to me—my struggle during the night and my achievement. I grabbed the pad and read, in a very clear if a trifle shaky writing, the following:

Chapter XII : The Dream

THE BANANA IS GREAT, BUT THE SKIN IS GREATER.

For a long time I lay there gazing in bewilderment at this strange statement, turning it over in my mind as I have done many times since. So this was the end of my search, the goal of my hard-won achievement, the answer to the timeless riddle of existence. I put down the pad as my boy came out on to the veranda with my *chota hazri* of tea, toast, and... a banana. As I removed the skin from the fruit I could not help feeling a pang of disappointment at this unexpected *denouement*, and I was sure that when Maung Ba Ohn heard of it he would only be quietly and inwardly amused.

Chapter XIII

THE WARNING

June drifted into July, and July into August. During these months I explored Mandalay and the surrounding country thoroughly and methodically. During the day I would wander far afield in my car, bumping leisurely over the rough roads, my eyes soothed and enchanted by the green of the rice-fields, the warmth of the sun-shine, and the good smell of the earth after rain. The little villages, with their cheerful, kindly inhabitants, were always an attraction to me. Many a happy afternoon did I laze away in the shade of a bamboo hut, sipping the warm, milky toddy, fresh from the top-most leaves of some tall tree, up which an agile villager had shinned like a monkey up a stick, his ankles bound together with rope and a leathern protector on his chest.

At other times I would visit the *hpongyis* in the little *hpongyi-kyaung* (monastery) across the way from my house. Here I would occasionally be invited to drink tea with the old *saya-gyi* (head-priest), a great honour, and with him I would discuss the Buddhist religion while the younger and more materially minded monks smiled and whispered in the background. I think that during those weeks I was very happy, very content, except, maybe, for an occasional misgiving that I was not doing anything, not getting anywhere. Had I been an Asiatic this would not have worried me, but I was a European and, much as I desired to steep and soak myself in this Eastern atmosphere, it was difficult completely to eradicate the inbred ideas and ideals of the West. But what I failed to achieve in the daylight I fancied I achieved in the dark.

Ah! Those nights, when I would wander through the byways of the city with Ba Ohn, visiting pagodas, attending *pwes* (dances), and searching out opium-dens. There was always some new sight to be seen, some new song to be heard, some new scent to be inhaled through widespread, quivering nostrils. I felt, somewhere deep within me, that I was living dangerously, but I was young and in love and did not heed. For when we finally came to rest in some little den, and stretched ourselves out on either side of the tray with the lamp, I knew that the first long intake from the carefully prepared pipe would wipe away these misgivings and leave me only with the words of Omar Khayyam:

Chapter XIII : The Warning 53

Unborn To-morrow and dead Yesterday,
Why fret about them if To-day be sweet!

But an incident occurred in July which gave me food for thought. I had driven up to Maymyo, the hill-station about forty miles away, on business, and Maung Ba Ohn had accompanied me. I had intended returning in the afternoon, but finding that I could not complete my business in time, decided to stay there the night and return the next day. I drove back to the rest-house in the evening to tell Ba Ohn of my change of plans. I found him waiting for me in a very strange state of agitation. His gay *gaungbaung* was awry and his long black hair dishevelled, but it was his face, his hands, and his speech which told me that something was definitely amiss. His hands, usually so eloquent, were as stammeringly agitated as his speech, while the ashen pallor of his thin face accentuated the look of dire distress in his dark eyes. 'Whatever is the matter with you, Ba Ohn?' I asked. 'I don't know this place, *thakin*,' he stammered. 'And I must have my smoke.' His evident distress was painful to witness, and every now and then he was seized with a fit of prodigious yawning, his mouth open wide until the white teeth stood bare against the stretched red line of the lips. I had seen men yawning like that when they arrived late at an opium-den for their evening smoke, and I knew what it meant; I knew that I could do nothing to help him. He ran off into the darkness as if the devil and all his kin were at his heels. Towards dawn he returned, sane and debonair as usual. Calm and peace had returned to his previously haggard eyes, and I knew that somewhere he had found a refuge from the terror that had overtaken him on the previous night. 'What was it, Ba Ohn?' I asked, a trifle anxiously. 'Oh, nothing, *thakin*,' he said. 'It has gone now. It comes when you cannot get your smoke. But one pipe and—pff! it is gone.' He smiled his strange, attractive smile, but I was not satisfied. 'But it doesn't come to me, Ba Ohn.' 'No,' he murmured softly, 'not yet, not yet.'

We were both very quiet as we drove down those hairpin bends which form the middle third of the Maymyo-Mandalay road. I was wondering what this terrible thing could be that metamorphoses the opium-smoker temporarily deprived of his smoke. I was now smoking almost nightly, but an occasional abstinence had not seemed to have had any noticeable effects. Perhaps it was not too late. I stole a glance at my companion as he sat beside me. Cool, elegant, almost exotic in his colouring and clothing, he looked a very different person from that distraught, dishevelled object of fear that had disappeared, moaning, into the darkness the evening before. 'Was it bad, Ba Ohn?' I asked. He knew what I meant. 'Pretty bad,' he answered quietly, and I shivered.

I questioned Ba Ohn more closely that evening as we lay smoking in a little den down by the river, but he either would not or could not be more explicit. I gathered, however, that it was a distress of both body and spirit, and that the bodily symptoms were mainly centred in the loins and thighs. Further inquiry was useless. Ba Ohn had his pipe, and the events of the previous night were, to him, a Dead Yesterday. Nevertheless, through my mind flitted thoughts of a terror of what some Unborn To-morrow might bring, and it took more pipes than usual, that night, before I could attain to even a semblance of peace of mind.

The next morning, as I sat in a long chair smoking a cheroot before breakfast, I reviewed the whole matter in my mind. When I had first smoked opium, after that chance encounter in the inner room of the Chinese eating-house, it had been curiosity, a desire for a new experience. I had continued because the atmosphere of the dens, the effects of the opium, and the personality of Ba Ohn and the other smokers had all interested and intrigued me. But at the back of my mind had always been the belief that, when I so desired, I could stop. Now this belief had been rudely shaken, and I felt the necessity, cost what it might, to put it to the test.

As I sat smoking and considering the matter my Chinese boy brought a card to me, and on it I read the name of a Captain and Adjutant in the Salvation Army. Thinking that he had called for a subscription, I asked him to come up. He entered, very neat in white uniform with red facings, with his book in his hand, but, on seeing me, he did a very curious thing. He forgot about his subscriptions, and, coming over to my chair, he said, 'Excuse me, but do you mind if I pray for your soul?' I was a bit taken aback, but managed to murmur, 'Not at all. It's very kind of you,' thinking that he would at least go and do it elsewhere. To my horror and the amazement of my boy, he went down on his knees by the side of my chair and began to pray aloud. I felt very uncomfortable, not knowing whether I should stand or remain as I was, but I could not help admiring the courage of the man. However, even these unsolicited prayers brought me little comfort in my dilemma. I knew that this matter must be faced by me, and by me alone, and that the success or failure of the issue should be determined by meditative reasoning within myself rather than by the counter-irritant of religious emotion.

As I rose to go in to breakfast I looked across the road and saw the yellow-robed monks and novices returning to the little monastery, their rice-filled begging-bowls clasped in front of them. That was the way, I thought to myself, the Middle Way. I would become a Buddhist priest.

Clear, very clear and distinct in the still morning air, came the monotonous intoning of the old *saya-gyi* at his early meditations:

Buddham saranam gissami
Dhammam saranam gissami.
Sangham saranam gissami.'
(I take refuge in Buddha.
I take refuge in his Law.
I take refuge in his Order.)

Perhaps here, in the Noble Order of the Yellow Robe, I too might find refuge from the terror that had begun to haunt me. Yes, I would put on the Yellow Robe, and in the paths of humility and abstinence would I seek sanctuary. My mind was made up; I returned to the dining-room where, from the top of my desk, my little old Buddha gazed down on me with his inscrutable eyes.

Chapter XIV

THE YELLOW ROBE (I)

Having made up my mind, I immediately set about putting my plans into execution. That same morning I drove down to the headquarters of a local Burmese Buddhist charitable organization, of which I was a member. With these kindly folk I had spent many a pleasant day visiting pagodas, almshouses, and *hpongyi-kyaungs* (monasteries) in and around Mandalay. It did not, therefore, come as any great surprise to them when I explained my mission. These Burmese Buddhists are a tolerant race, as all true Buddhists should be, and, although unaware of the real motive underlying my action, they were too courteous to be openly inquisitive. Indeed, they were overjoyed that one of their number, though nominally not a Buddhist, should thus crown his interest in their religion by his desire to wear, for a time, the Yellow Robe. After a long and excited discussion it was decided that I should enter the Ma-soe-yin-kyaung-daik, a monastery in the heart of Mandalay, whose *saya-gyi* was a man of wide erudition and great piety.

In the afternoon we drove down to the monastery and drew up outside the main gate. Removing our shoes and slippers, we entered a large, tree-shaded courtyard, in the middle of which was a well and around which were several *kyaungs* (buildings), on the stone steps and plinths of which were seated a number of yellow-robed monks. As we made our way towards one of these buildings I looked round me with interest at this, the setting for a new experience. Everything about me seemed to exhale an atmosphere of peace and security. Several dogs lay basking in the sun, while fowls pecked in the dust or roosted in the branches of the trees. Life was sacred within the precincts of a monastery, and these fowls, I knew, had been placed there by pious Burmans as due reward for services faithfully rendered during their egg-laying maturity. The golden and orange yellow of the monks' robes made a vivid splash of colour against the white stone of the steps and plinths, while from within the dark teak-wood halls, like the somnolent droning of many bees, came the sounds of other monks at their meditations.

In company with my two Burmese friends I passed up the steps of one of these buildings on the left of the courtyard and entered a large, spacious hall, the roof of which was supported by red and gold lacquered teak pillars. Round the wall, their doors opening out on to the central hall, were little cubicles or cells, the interiors of which were lighted and ventilated by small, barred windows. At one end of the hall stood an immense figure of Buddha, and in front of this were many bunches of flowers scenting the room with their heavy, sweet perfume. One corner of this end of the hall was partitioned off to form a large cubicle with a small anteroom, and it was in this anteroom that we waited until the *saya-gyi* should be ready to receive us. 'Another Inner Room!' I thought to myself, with a vague prayer that the curiosity that had led me to it would have a more satisfactory outcome.

A few minutes later the door slid back and a pleasant, smiling young novice beckoned to us to enter. The room in which we found ourselves was some twelve feet by nine, bare of furniture except for the many shelves of books which lined the wall. On a low platform sat U Nyana, the head priest of the particular *kyaung* and the man we had come forth to see. U Nyana was, at that time, in his early forties, and had been in the priesthood since his nineteenth year. Constant meditation and strict attention to his scholastic and monastic duties had withered his body, but on his face and in his eyes was that look of serenity and understanding that can only be acquired by those who have fought against the desires of the body and overcome them.

We sat cross-legged on the rush mat before him while my friend explained our errand. He listened gravely and then addressed me in fair English, 'Why do you want to join the Sangha (Order)?' he asked. 'I am a seeker, *Saya-gyi*,' I replied. He considered this for a minute or two and seemed to be satisfied. 'And what do you know of the Dharma (Law)?' he asked. I told him that I had studied books on Buddhism, but that I was anxious to learn more, and that was one of the reasons for my presence there. Yes, he said thoughtfully, it could be arranged, but there would have to be a certain amount of preliminary preparation. I should have to attend there every afternoon for instruction, and when he was satisfied that I was ready he would fix the day for my ordination. 'How long will that be, *Saya-gyi*?' I asked, a little anxiously. 'Is it so urgent, then?' he countered, a grave smile on his pale lips. 'It is somewhat urgent,' I answered. 'Ah! Then we will do our best,' he said. 'But it may be a month.' I sighed a little, but there was that in his face which told me that here I should find a wise and understanding teacher. It was with a lighter heart and a glimmer of hope that I left that dark little inner room and passed out into the blinding glare of the courtyard. I felt that if I failed to find refuge here under such a teacher the fault would be mine, and mine alone.

That same evening I told Ba Ohn my plans as we lay smoking in Ah Hpan's den at the House of the Deer. He looked very thoughtful, but made no comment until I had finished.

'The idea is good,' he said. 'By the wearing of the Yellow Robe for even one day you will acquire more merit than in many years as a layman, but—how long does the *thakin* intend to stay in the Sangha?' 'God knows!' I replied; and, by the slight twitching at the corners of his mouth, I felt that Ba Ohn too could make a pretty good guess.

During the ensuing week I moved my belongings from the bungalow near the Fort to a stone house in the Shoemakers' Quarter of the city. It was more conveniently situated for my daily visits to the monastery, and, though I would not admit it, for my nightly visits to the opium-dens. Every afternoon I would literally sit at the feet of U Nyana and listen while he discoursed on the tenets of Buddhism. With my notebook on the floor in front of me, I would take down page after page of the formulae of meditation in Pali, the language of the priests. All of these I had to learn off by heart, and, most difficult of all, I had to learn the priestly way of intoning the Three Refuges, thrice repeated, in that deep, vibrant monotone which I had heard so often and which has to be performed without any motion of the lips. Then there were the two hundred and seventy odd rules which a monk had to observe, but of these, I was glad to see, U Nyana only insisted on my memorizing the more important. It was hard work, and my *saya-gyi* was no easygoing taskmaster; but it was interesting, and, there being much at stake, I proved a moderately apt pupil and made good progress. The time came at length when even U Nyana was satisfied, and a day late in September was fixed for my ordination. The night before the ceremony I smoked a last pipe with Ba Ohn. As I lay watching him manipulating the pellets on the end of his long needle he seemed to epitomize all the worldly desires which I was about to give up. He himself, however, was unmoved. 'To-morrow night,' he said, 'I shall smoke alone, but if you need me, *thakin,* you know where to find me.' So I left him, in that back room of the House of the Deer, while I went forth to make a bid for freedom before it was too late, if it were not already too late.

Chapter XV

THE YELLOW ROBE (II)

It was about eleven o'clock the next morning that I arrived outside the gates of the monastery, and, unlacing and removing my shoes, entered the courtyard. The serene optimism induced by the opium of the previous night had given place to a vague sense of foreboding and loneliness, but the scene inside the great hall quickly stimulated my interest. My friends of the Buddhist charitable association had turned up in full force, complete with their wives, their sons, and their daughters. The women had been there since early morning, feeding the monks and preparing a feast for themselves and their friends.

It was a gay sight. At one end of the hall were low, round lacquered tables at which squatted groups of gaily apparelled, smiling-faced humanity, while at the other end were small knots of serene-eyed, yellow-robed monks, who seldom seemed to raise their voices above a whisper. To and fro between these two contrasting groups flitted the younger members of the laity, bearing in their hands water and towels so that their elders and betters might cleanse the hand with which they had been eating. I stood for a moment watching this friendly, happy little garden of human flowers. What a kindly, tolerant race of people these Burmese were! Many of them knew of my hidden trouble, but they were too gentle and understanding to judge. Instead, they had busied themselves since dawn in the hope, and sure hope, that the knowledge of their love and affection would make this, the first step on a difficult path, easier.

The ceremony was to commence at noon, and shortly before that time the tables and other impedimenta were removed. As the five head-priests, who were to officiate, entered, the whole company bowed themselves to the ground. The *hpongyis*, one of whom was U Nyana, were presided over by the head of the Queen's monastery, a venerable old man who had been a monk when Theebaw ruled in Mandalay. The five seated themselves cross-legged on the floor along one side of the hall, and in front of them I placed my gifts, as is the custom on such occasions. There were sets of yellow robes, leather sandals, long-handled sunshades, writing material, and many varieties of fruit. The ceremony of the handing over of these gifts was considerably shortened by an act of symbolism; instead of each article being presented separately, they were handed over *en masse* through the pouring of water from one vessel to another while the requisite formula was recited. Meanwhile I was sitting on my heels facing the priests and on the other side of the gifts, feeling rather nervous and very uncomfortable. This squatting posture, natural to the Asiatic, is very trying to a European, especially when it has to be maintained for any length of time, and I knew that I should be very stiff before we had finished.

The presentation of the gifts being completed, there followed my introduction to the assembled board. Two of my elderly Burmese friends, devout men and of good repute, acted as my sponsors, while U Nyana spoke of my spiritual progress under his tuition and my evident desire for knowledge. As I sat there, my hands together and my head sunk between my knees, I felt a little ashamed that I had not been more frank with him, and I resolved there and then to unburden my soul to him at the earliest opportunity. The monks, having satisfied themselves as to the worthiness of my desire to enter the Sangha, called on me to repeat the formulae of meditation. This was the crucial part of my examination, much importance being attached to the shade of inflexion given to each syllable. But I knew them. Had I not gone over them, time and time again, with Ba Ohn as we lay smoking during those long, hot nights in Ah Hpan's den? They tripped off my tongue, easily, fluently, even as they do sometimes now when I am worried, and they can still bring me a measure of that peace which I have so long sought.

As the last Pali words, expressing a desire that any merit which might have been acquired by my meditations should be shared by the whole world, fell from my lips, I rose from my cramped position and was led away to the antechamber of U Nyana's apartment. Here I undressed, and a barber lathered and shaved my head until I felt very, very naked. My assistants then proceeded to invest me in the yellow robes. One of these, wrapped round the waist, is held in place by a yellow cord. The other is worn about the upper part of the body, leaving the right shoulder bare except when begging. Neither garment has any stitching, and even when, with Occidental instinct, I desired to retain my handkerchief, my assistants had to remove the hem before handing it to me. A string of wooden beads was placed in my hand, and before returning to the hall I took a survey of the remainder of my equipment. This consisted of a black-lacquered begging-bowl, a yellow webbing sling for it, a pair of leather sandals, a palm-leaf fan, a long, black-handled paper sunshade, a filter, needle and thread.

Chapter XV : The Yellow Robe (II)   61

Feeling very strange, but unaccountably serene, I returned to the hall and bowed myself before the head-priests. I was conscious of a subdued murmur from the gay company on my left, but did not turn my head. It was as if some sense of aloofness had entered my soul even while I had put on my body the garments of renunciation. In response to a request from the head of the Queen's monastery, I repeated the Three Refuges three times in the sonorous, vibrant intoning only used by the monks. I sensed that the eyes of the five priests were fixed on my mouth, but my lips never moved. As a sign of their approval I was invited to join them and took up my seat, cross-legged, on the right of the line.

Then followed the interesting, but somewhat embarrassing, procedure of choosing for me a Pali name by which I should be known as long as I remained in the Sangha. A lengthy conversation took place between my sponsors, U Nyana, and the other monks, in which my particular characteristics were fully and openly discussed. I kept my eyes on the ground, pretending neither to hear nor to understand, but I could not help feeling a flush, born of mingled pleasure and shame, rise to the crown of my newly shaven head. At length the venerable old head of the Queen's monastery held up his hand and informed the assembled company that I was to be known as U Nipuna, the Gentle Monk, and with that the ceremony came to an end.

The head-priests rose and walked in single file towards the door, and I put my hands together before my face and bowed to the floor as they passed. It was not until after their departure that I fully realized to what heights the preceding ceremony had raised me in the estimation of my Burmese friends. It was time, too, for them to go, but before departing they came and prostrated themselves before me. The elders and their wives, the handsome young men and the oh, so attractive young women—these friends of mine with whom I had laughed and played and eaten but yesterday came and bowed themselves in reverence before me, and I felt as though some physical barrier had arisen between us... and my heart ached.

Soon they were gone, and I was left alone in that vast, empty hall. It was nearing sunset, and as I sat there idly clicking my beads I thought that now was the time when the little oil-lamps would be coming to life in the opium-dens of the city. Ba Ohn would have to smoke alone to-night. A feeling of nausea came over me, an almost irresistible impulse to throw off these yellow robes and to run through the dusk back to Ba Ohn and the House of the Deer. I rose abruptly to my feet, as if to put the impulse into effect, and caught sight of the large white figure of the Buddha at the end of the hall. I walked towards it, my bare feet moving noiselessly over the floor. There were lighted candles before the figure, and the air was heavy with the scent of the flowers. I gazed up at this representation of the All-wise and All-compassionate One. He had shown me a Way, and an Eight-fold Path, and here was I thinking of turning aside before I had even set foot on it. I sank down to the ground and prostrated myself before the figure. My beads began to click through my fingers, and as the darkness fell I began to repeat the Three Refuges:

Buddham saranam gissami.
Dhammam saranam gissami.
Sangham saranam gissami.

Chapter XVI

THE YELLOW ROBE (III)

My meditations were interrupted by the sound of a wooden clapper-gong in the courtyard. Row upon row of yellow-clad figures began to take up their positions before the Buddha, and I slipped quietly away to the back of the hall, where in the gloom I seated myself at the end of the last line, as became my position as the most recently joined member of the community. When all were seated U Nyana came out from his room and took his place at the head of his monks. Then in unison the whole assembly began to intone the formulæ which I had been at such pains to learn. It was a wonderful, an awe-inspiring experience—the vast hall, the illuminated figure of the Lord Buddha, the scent of the flowers, the row upon row of yellow-robed monks gradually merging into the gloom at the back of the hall, and, above all, the deep, soul-stirring vibrations of the Three Refuges as they emanated from the motionless lips of that shaven multitude. The world seemed very far away at that moment, and I felt that my spirit was being borne along on that vibrating wave towards a Nirvana far more desirable than the ephemeral bliss so easy, so fatally easy, to attain in the House of the Deer.

After the monks had dispersed for the night, some to continue their meditations, some to study in their little cubicles, U Nyana invited me to his room. Here I carried out my resolution, taken during the ordination ceremony, and told him of my troubles and fears. He heard me out with attention and sympathy, but passed no judgment. It was, he said, a matter which concerned myself alone. He could show me the Way, a way which he himself had had to tread when the desire for the illusory pleasures of this world was strong upon him. He had joined the Sangha at the age of nineteen, an age, I knew, at which the blood of the young Burman flows hottest through his veins. The road was not easy, he said, and as I looked at his emaciated figure and ascetic features I knew that it had not been easy, even for him. He advocated steadfastness and perseverance on the path on which I had set my feet, but told me that, should the call of that other world prove too strong for me, there was nothing to hold me back from it. I had joined the Sangha of my own free will; I was at liberty to leave it when I so desired. The matter rested entirely with myself. He would instruct me in the Law, as became a *saya-gyi*, and, in order that I might have easy access to him at any time, he would allow me to use his antechamber instead of one of the ordinary cells. It was nearly midnight when I left U Nyana, and his eyes were very kind on parting. I knew that he was right; the evolution of my soul lay in my own hands, and, apart from example and precept, he could do little to aid me in the matter. I would not have had it otherwise. As I sow, I said in my pride, so am I content to reap. It was natural, it was just, it was... inevitable.

That night I slept, my robes wrapped around me, under one of the trees in the monastery garden. I was awakened at dawn by the crowing of a jungle cock in the branches overhead. 'Cock-a-doodle-errhp!' There was no mistaking that call, with its abrupt ending. I had heard it many times in the jungles of Northern Burma and had often wondered why the call should differ so from the 'Cock-a-doodle-doooo' of the domestic fowl. Now, as I looked up through the branches, the reason became obvious. These fowls, placed in the sanctuary of the garden by their devout owners, had grown their wings and taken to roosting in the trees, and even as I watched I saw one old cock stretch himself for his morning call. 'Cock-a-doodle-do—' he began, and as he stretched out his neck to finish he nearly over-balanced but just managed to pull himself up with a sudden '—errhp.' Of course, that final long-drawn-out 'doooo' was practicable when one was on the ground and could take a step or two forward in order to preserve one's balance, but on a branch of a tree it was another matter. Again, while it was perfectly safe in this garden for a cock to lose his balance and have to fly to the ground, it was quite another matter for the real jungle cock perched safely above the morning mists of a hostile jungle. But this was no time for ornithological study. There was a feeling of uncommon emptiness in my stomach, and I realized that I had eaten nothing since the previous morning; also I knew that if I wanted to fill that emptiness the sooner I started on my begging round the better.

I rose and went over to one of the wells from which I drew up a bucketful of clear, cold water. Three or four other young monks were gathered round the well, and with their assistance I managed to carry out a satisfactory ablution without offending against the proprieties. They were kindly folk, these smooth-voiced, smooth-faced, almost effeminate-looking *hpongyis*, and nothing was too much trouble for them. With their help and advice, I adjusted my upper robe in the intricate fashion prescribed for begging, so that only the head, hands, and feet were visible. Then, with bare feet and downcast eyes, my black begging-bowl clasped in front of me, I started out on my first begging round.

Chapter XVI : The Yellow Robe (III)

All Buddhist monks, with the exception of the *saya-gyis* and the very old *hpongyis,* beg daily for their food. The Burmese house-wives, who are usually very devout, prepare each morning a bowl of rice, according to their means, for the feeding of the monks. This ceremony

> *is twice bless'd;*
> *It blesseth him that gives and him that takes.*

In the priest there is instilled the humility of which the Lord Buddha is their great example. The laity, on the other hand, acquire merit by their action, and the acquisition of merit is the principal part of the life of a Burmese woman. The monks usually have their own houses of call, where they are known, but this is not necessary. During the begging round the priest does not speak, neither does he raise his eyes from the ground. He approaches a house and stops outside the door, but still facing the way in which he is proceeding. The lady of the house will then put a large spoonful of rice into the begging-bowl, and without a word the monk passes on. Should the housewife have exhausted her stock of rice she will shikoe and ask for forgiveness, but the monk will pass on as before.

I found this part of the day a little trying, as the round was not usually over till half-past eight or nine, by which time the sun was well up, and my bare and shaven head invited sunstroke. The ground also was very rough, and I was devoutly thankful for the rule prescribing that the eyes should be kept fixed on the ground in front of me, as I was thus enabled to avoid any excrescence which might otherwise have damaged my feet. Some of the more elderly monks would be accompanied by a little boy who carried the bowl for them on a bamboo rod borne on his shoulder and counterbalanced at the other end by a tray with little china dishes for offerings of curry, etc. The *saya-gyis* were usually in receipt of an allowance of rice, oil, etc., from the founder and builder of the *Kyaung* or other charitable sources.

I had no difficulty in getting my bowl filled that morning. All my friends who had been present at my initiation the day before were expecting me, and many and varied were the little tit-bits which began to encircle the central pile of snowy rice. Such embarrassment as I may have experienced at the beginning of the round soon passed away. The early morning air was cool, and the feel of the dust was pleasant under my feet. Also, I was very hungry, and as the savoury odours of curries and rice rose to the nostrils of my bent head I began to take a very material interest in each offering. As the sun rose, so the bowl filled, until there was hardly room for another chilli, and I retraced my steps to the monastery.

Arriving there, I replaced my robe in its normal position and joined the other monks in the great hall. I was already accustomed to eating with my fingers when visiting the houses of my Burmese friends, and this provided no difficulties. The rice was still warm and very palatable. When I had satisfied my immediate hunger I put the rest aside to be eaten cold just before noon. One of the principal rules which had to be observed was that no food was to be eaten after midday.

In the period between the two morning meals the monks would wander from *kyaung* to *kyaung*, so that they might see exactly what lectures were to be given by the *saya-gyis* that day. These were posted up on a notice-board in each *kyaung*, and the monks were at liberty to attend any lecture they desired.

These lectures would take place during the afternoon and were delivered by the *saya-gyis*—in this case U Nyana—from the raised dais in front of the antechamber. The monks, equipped with notebooks and pencils, would arrange themselves in rows on the floor before the dais. The courses of instruction were exceedingly thorough, the lecturer illustrating his remarks by means of blackboard and chalk. When not attending these lectures I used to sit at the feet of U Nyana in his private room while he instilled into me the many rules which a Buddhist priest had to observe. At other times he would talk to me of the past, of the days when he first joined the Sangha, and of the consequent struggle against temptation which he had endured. As I looked at his frail body and ascetic features I could see embodied there the physical cost and spiritual reward of that ordeal, which must have been especially exacting to a young and devout Burman who nevertheless loved life with the inherent capacity of his charming, happy-go-lucky race.

During the afternoon some of the monks would pay visits to the pagodas, particularly the venerable Arakan Pagoda, or Paya Gyi, of which I was extremely fond. One of the most vivid memories which I possess is of the main shrine of the Arakan Pagoda between midnight and dawn of a night of the full moon. The iron gates of the shrine are drawn back, and the immense figure of the Lord Buddha, brilliantly illuminated by electric light and thousands of candles, stands revealed to the assembly. This is the figure which was blessed by the Lord Buddha himself, and was subsequently the cause of many wars between Burma and Arakan, until it was finally carried off by the Burmese and conveyed the hundreds of miles to Mandalay, along a road especially cut through the jungle and over the mountains for that purpose. The robes of the figure are thickly coated with gold-leaf, bought from the stalls and offered by the people to the monks

3. Robinson as a Buddhist monk

in attendance, and the never-to-be-forgotten scent of the pagoda flowers pervades the whole shrine.

At other times I would leave the central shrine and wander out into the Courtyard of the Sacred Fish. This was an immense concrete tank in which lived every variety of fish, ranging from very small ones to huge turtles. This tank always fascinated me. The pagoda slaves, beautiful girls from Arakan, sold bread to the devout sightseers, and when this was thrown in the whole pool surged and bubbled as though it were some mighty cauldron. It was a horrible sight, and one could not help wondering what would happen to anyone luckless enough to fall in.

As twilight fell, however, I began to feel an uneasiness creep over me, and I grew very restless. This was the time of day I dreaded most—the time when the little oil-lamps were being lit in the opium-dens all over the city. Sometimes I would seek out U Nyana and with him discuss feverishly points of doctrine or comparative religion. He knew in what distress I was and was always very gentle and very patient. So we would talk until the sound of the clapper-bell summoned us to the evening meditations, and there in the dimly lit hall, soothed by the vibrations of many voices intoning as one, I would find peace for twenty-four hours.

The days passed peacefully enough in their ordered routine: the rising at dawn and the ablutions at the well, the begging round in the cool of the early morning, and the studies and lectures in the afternoon. But that terrible restlessness at dusk showed no signs of diminishing. U Nyana saw how heavy I was finding the strain, and, calling me to his room one evening, he advised me to leave Mandalay for a time and wander further afield through the villages in the surrounding countryside. The advice seemed good to me; it was possible that a change of environment would distract my mind from this obsession which haunted me. Accordingly, very early the next morning, I slung my begging-bowl round my shoulder, and, with leather sandals on my feet and fan and sunshade in my hand, I took to the road.

The sun rose, and after an hour or two I began to feel hot and hungry with the unaccustomed exercise. There was a village some little way ahead, so I stopped and prepared my robes for begging. This was rather awkward as it entailed stuffing my sunshade, fan, and sandals into the cord round my waist, but, as all were concealed by my upper garment, it did not matter. There were very few monks about, but the appearance of this stranger in their midst excited the curiosity of the villagers. It was then that I experienced the feeling of humility for which

Chapter XVI : The Yellow Robe (III)   69

the Buddha prescribed the begging-bowl as a symbol. At Mandalay I had been known personally at every house of call and the round had been made pleasant and easy by the charity of my friends. Here it was another matter: I was a stranger, and the villagers were not as well-to-do as their city cousins, but Burmese women are always charitable to the monks, whatever their means and wherever they may be. Do they not spend their whole lives in the acquisition of merit, so that, in their next reincarnation, they may be fortunate enough to be born as men? And these villages were as hospitable as their means would allow, but it was with a begging-bowl very far from full that I squatted down to eat my morning meal. However, I rinsed my bowl and quenched my thirst in a near-by stream and went on my way.

I stayed that night in a little *hpongyi-kyaung* among some paddy-fields and was very kindly received by the monks. They were naturally very curious about me and asked me many questions, but I was uneasy in mind and body and not very communicative. So I passed from village to village, and ever this thing pursued me. My begging-bowl was seldom full, and the heat and the length of my marches began to tell on me. I grew very thin, and then, one day in October, when I had halted for the night at a little riverside village, I gave in and went aboard a steamer which happened to be moored along-side. I had no money (I was not allowed to carry money), but a charitable fellow-traveller acquired merit by assisting me. The boat arrived at Mandalay that afternoon, and I made my way at once to the Ma-soe-yin-kyaung-daik.

U Nyana was in his room, at work on his Pali dictionary, when I entered. He knew at once that I had failed, that I had been unable to break the bonds that held me, that I was going back. He did not remonstrate with me; he did not say a word as I bowed myself to the earth before him for the last time, but his eyes were very kind.

I had none of my own clothes there, but U Nyana pointed to some Burmese clothing in a corner of his room. Passing into the antechamber, I removed my yellow robes and hastily donned the silken *lungyi*, vest, and Burmese coat. Then, binding the gay *gaungbaung* round my head to hide my shaven scalp, I slipped out into the night. As I passed through the courtyard the monastery bell sounded the call to meditation, and one of the many pariah dogs sat up on his haunches and howled. A dog that howls at the sounding of the temple bell, I mused, will be reborn a man. This was an old Burmese superstition, but it sent a shiver down my spine. What of me? I thought, as I slunk through the gateway and headed for the House of the Deer.

On arrival I passed swiftly through the main smoking-room and turned right to the little room which I had known so well in the past. Maung Ba Ohn was there, smoking alone. I threw myself down on the other side of the tray. He looked up at me, a curious light in his brilliant eyes. 'Ah!' he breathed softly, 'So the *thakin* has come back. I wondered how long...' He did not finish the sentence, but, fixing a pill in the pipe, handed the mouthpiece over to me. I think that he saw, from the look on my face, that further comment would be out of place—at least for the present.

Chapter XVII

SLAVES OF THE LAMP

After two or three pipes my tautened muscles and nerves relaxed. That terrible feeling of uneasiness fell away from me, and I stretched out my limbs in an ecstasy of well-being and contentment. My bid for freedom had been pitifully futile, my fall from grace all the greater for the heights to which I had aspired. I had thought to escape; I had thought to find refuge in the Noble Order of the Yellow Robe, but the chains that held me had been too strong and I had been very weak. It seemed to me then that I had gained little by the bitter struggle of the past week; but this was not the case, and the time was to come when the simple beliefs of those kindly Buddhist monks were to stand me in very good stead. But at that moment it seemed to me that I had gained nothing and lost everything. It seemed hopeless to struggle, and, after all, I thought, why should one struggle? Through the open door of the little room I could see other smokers, their yellow and brown faces lit by the light of the little lamps. Smooth, peaceful faces with unwrinkled foreheads and drooping eyelids. Their voices, too, were subdued and soothing. In fact, to a casual observer they were, in these two respects, not unlike the yellow-robed monks of the Ma-soe-yin-kyaung-daik, but I knew the difference, and knew that those foreheads would only remain smooth and unwrinkled as long as the cotton-seed oil filled the lamps and opium the little wooden cups. I knew it and they knew it, but while there was money to foot the bill we never spoke of it.

> *Unborn To-morrow and dead Yesterday,*
> *Why fret about them if To-day be sweet!*

Yes, life seemed very sweet to us when the lamps were lit, the wicks trimmed, and the opium pills gurgling pleasantly over all. From our lofty, remote plane we viewed the world abstractedly, dispassionately. In such circumstances we felt that we could gaze down even into the Pit with equanimity.

It was late that night when I left the House of the Deer and made my way through the darkness to my house. As I strode through the narrow, silent lanes I came to the conclusion that, for the time being, it was useless to fight against these intangible bonds which held so fast my body and soul. For a time at least I should have to admit defeat, until an opportunity arose for a final effort.

The house which I had taken near the Shoemakers' Quarter was a two-storeyed building. The ground floor was occupied by my landlord, his wife, and an old hag who appeared to be the wife's aunt. The landlord was one Maung Ba Maung, the off-spring of a Chinaman and a Burmese woman, a merry fellow who boasted of what the Burmese euphemistically term a 'private wife' in another quarter of the city. His legitimate wife was a tall creature, fascinating in her way, but very religious. I rented the upper half of the house, and this was approached by a staircase and a heavily barred trap-door. The apartments were simplicity itself: a large room, further subdivided by two inner rooms, ventilated by wooden Venetian shutters. There was an open balcony in front and a bath-place at the back. One of these two inner rooms I had fitted up as a bedroom; the other I now decided to transform into a smoking-den *par excellence*.

These inner rooms were some nine feet by eighteen feet and allowed me plenty of scope for my imagination. The room which I had assigned for smoking was on the right as one emerged through the trap-door. At one end I had inserted a wooden platform of the usual height of about eighteen inches and of some six feet in depth. Round the walls I hung three or four scroll Chinese paintings. The boards of the platform were covered with Oriental rugs of a corresponding shade, and at the foot of the platform were hung deep red velvet curtains, some nine feet in height, which could be drawn across at will. In a wall-cupboard by the side of the platform were a variety of opium pipes, lamps, needles, utensils, and scrapers.

It was an ideal smoking-den, soothing to the eye, with everything that an opium-smoker could desire. There were even little packets of musk, which sweetens the pipe so that the air becomes fragrant with the scent instead of merely heavy and fuggy. The lamp-shades were painted in attractive Chinese designs with women and trees and birds and little bridges. The pipes ranged from the most common and the best bamboo pipes to the more expensive ivory ones with jade mouthpieces. There were tea sets—those quaint wicker-work sets with their handle-less cups and cane-handled tea-pots. There was everything there, from the horn-pots containing the opium to the slim green packets enclosing the cocaine. For use with the latter were a small brass box containing the lime and a little brass spatula for applying the lime and cocaine to the lower lip. Although it is not usual for an opium-smoker to take to cocaine, this latter drug was often in evidence in the dens of Mandalay. There were two or three ways by which it could be obtained. Firstly, there were the so-called medical halls where the three-cornered brown bottles, the product of reputable British firms, could be bought at a price; secondly, there were the slim green packets obtainable, if you knew where, for the small sum of eight annas or so. Again there were the men who sold openly in the market-place. These sellers of 'pan' would occasionally mix a little cocaine with their goods, and then the betel-nut, which normally cost only a fraction of a penny, would cost you eight annas or even a rupee.

It was easy to distinguish the cocaine-addict from the opium-smoker. The latter were a slow-speaking, slow-moving, benign people, while the former were quick—quick of eye, quick of movement, and feverishly quick of speech—with dank hair and beads of sweat on the forehead. They did not sniff the cocaine through the nose as they do in the West. That would, to them, have been a waste. They smeared the lower lip with lime, and when the outer delicate tissue had been burned away they would apply the cocaine on the same spatulated instrument. As the drug took effect on the subcutaneous tissue the lips would be rubbed together, and the addict, imagining his lips to have assumed negroid proportions, would pout and blow so that he might attain reflex sensations from the benumbed vibrations. That is how it was, and I know because I have tried it many times, but never did cocaine obtain the same hold on me as opium.

This opium is another matter. It is the strongest, the most insidious, drug of all. It has been commercialized in many forms, but it is in the smoke that its most potent web is woven. Body and soul it will claim you and hold you, and, should you for any reason fail in your allegiance, it will cast you forth, racked and tortured in every fibre of your being, until death itself comes to you as a merciful release. I know, I know! But don't imagine that I write this in the hope that my tale will be anything more than a warning to those who read it.

Chapter XVIII

PLAGUE IN MANDALAY

For six months, during the cold weather of 1923-24, I made no further fight against the smoking of opium. Every evening, about half-past six, I used to adjourn to the inner room which I had fitted out for that purpose. Although I could by now manipulate the needle and pipe myself, I usually had a companion, and that companion was usually Maung Ba Ohn. He lived in an adjacent street, and sometimes he would bring with him a little boy, Ba Set, a cousin of his. Ba Set was some ten or twelve years old. His face was not handsome, but very pleasing in its ugliness, with eyes set well apart and a mouth rather over-stocked with teeth. The boy had a heart of gold and, for some unaccountable reason, became very attached to me. He was very well made, with very expressive hands and slits of eyes. When he smiled, however, which was rarely, his mouth was anything but a slit. Hour after hour this neat, trim little figure would sit, cross-legged, on the platform by my side while I smoked. Sometimes he would dance for me at the far end of the little room, and then the grace of his movements made one forget the honest ruggedness of his countenance. He never smoked, of course. I think that in his quiet way he would have done anything for me, within or without reason. I have to mention little Ba Set here because he meant a great deal to me in the trying months that were to follow, and if I am sure of anything in this life it is that he must have acquired lasting merit by his unswerving love and loyalty to me. When the time came that all others forsook me and fled, Ba Set alone remained.

When bubonic plague made its first sinister appearance in Mandalay about November of that year 1923, Ba Set was one of the few who accompanied me to the dispensary for inoculation. The Burmese dislike inoculation, and even the offer of an eight-anna reward fails to bring many to the doctor when plague is due to appear. Instead, there is a steady exodus from the city, mainly towards the east, but of those who remain many thousands fall victims to this infection. Before the British occupation smallpox used to be the chief scourge of Burma, but this disease has gradually been eliminated, though, with the increase of trade at the ports, bubonic plague crept in. As it always occurs during the cold weather the Burmese are apt to put it down to the presence of regal or viceregal visitors, who, naturally enough, plan their visits to the country during this period. That cold weather was bad. The inoculation which I received was so potent that for three days I was semi-conscious, a raving lunatic. Not that I was dangerous, but during the day I would hear myself eulogizing aloud over a certain Arabella to a circle of astonished but very courteous Burmese friends. I had never known, and had no desire to know, anyone of the name of Arabella. But there it was.

After two or three days this lunacy passed, and I was able to watch, by the light of the little lamps, the rapid passage of death through the native quarter. It was swift, inexorable. There was the old Chinaman who ran a tea-stall outside my house in the Shoemakers' Quarter. I had wished him well as one evening I left for the House of the Deer. On my return, in the early hours of the morning, he was dead. Another night I watched by the bed of a beautiful Burmese girl while injections were being made into the buboes in her armpits by a Burmese doctor, an old friend of mine. Funereal processions with their white-clad attendants and wailing women were constantly passing along the street. Every morning I would, unconsciously, inspect my armpits and groins for any signs of the tell-tale swellings. Little wonder that we smoked hard and played hard during those dark days. In the big open space of the outer room in my apartment my Burmese friends would meet for dancing or a game of *le-gaung-gyin*. This is a kind of crown-and-anchor, but played with an ivory top on which were engraved a snake, a cock, a pig, and a scorpion. The game was illegal, but the trapdoor leading from the ground floor made everything safe from surprise. Sometimes also I would engage a well-known dancing-girl to entertain my guests. One such occasion remains very vivid in my mind.

Her name was National Kin Thaung, and she was to the Burmese youth what a Hollywood star is to the average filmgoer of today. She was not, in my opinion, beautiful, but her dancing was certainly magnificent. Surrounded by two half-circles of her gaping, hot-blooded admirers and the members of her orchestra, she seemed the embodiment of charm as I watched her through the Venetian shutters of my little room where I was smoking with Ba Ohn. In one corner, near the band, sat U Shwe, an elderly old reprobate who was—shall we say?—the protector of National Kin Thaung. He too had been young in his time, many years ago, and did not like the looks which my younger guests were casting at the dancer. I felt that something might happen at any minute, so I summoned the girl into my room and told little Ba Set to go out and dance. National Kin Thaung was amusing, but U Shwe was very jealous and insisted that he must take her home. I agreed and offered to drive them both back in my car. We passed through the trap-door and out into the street. There was a large water-jar near the front door, and as we passed this a young lad, about seventeen years old, sprang out and tried to accost National Kin Thaung. I knew him well and knew him to be, under normal circumstances, a very decent boy. But the old man was very annoyed, and as I tried to soothe him I could not help thinking that he might have fared worse had he been on the North-east Frontier.

When I returned to my house I could hear, by the din, that something was amiss. I rushed upstairs and pushed up the trap-door. An amazing sight met my eyes. There was a free fight in progress between the band and my guests; the weapons were those most deadly of weapons, empty mineral-water bottles. I had no idea of the cause of the dispute, but, knowing the Burmese, guessed that it had to do with the approachability of National Kin Thaung. My appearance instantly quietened the uproar, and after making their apologies the combatants withdrew.

Such were the means by which we kept away the thought of the plague in Mandalay. Many is the time that, lying in a long cane chair, I have watched a rat cross the room, falter in its stride, and die. Then it was that I used to think of the flea, the plague flea, which, finding its host dead, would attach itself to a human being if there were no other rodent available. But my evening smoke, my nightly pills, and that curious impersonal outlook on life which I had imbibed as a Buddhist monk kept me free of worry.

One night I remember well when I had gone down to the House of the Deer to smoke with Ba Ohn. The little private room was, for some reason, occupied, and we had to take up our positions in the common den. Maung Ba Ohn had been there before me, and as I lay down opposite him I knocked against the back of the man who formed my opposite number in the pair. He was shrouded in a long cloth, but his friend, I could see, was making the pills. 'That man sleeps well,' I remarked to Ba Ohn. 'Yes,' he said quietly, 'He died half an hour ago from the plague. They are waiting to take him away.' It took a minute or two for the significance of this remark to filter through my opium-sodden mind. 'Dead?' I mused. 'So he is dead!' And that was all. I stretched out my hand for the pipe and... it was as nothing.

The curious hiatus between the receipt of information and the apprehension of it is peculiar to the opium smoker. There was an occasion once, about this time, when I was smoking with Ba Ohn in my own private room. Lying as I was on my right side, my left hand was placed on my left hip, and on the small finger of my left hand was a solid gold ring,

Chapter XVIII : Plague in Mandalay

manufactured from those nuggets which I had brought down from the North-east Frontier. As I smoked a young lad came into the room and began to talk to us. I knew him by sight, and it was not out of the way to see such a one there, but as he talked he began to twist my ring about the little finger of my left hand. From my position as I smoked I watched him doing this. I watched him remove the ring from my finger, and watched him leave the room, but it was not until he had been gone about five minutes that I realized that my ring had been stolen. I sent out to find him, but by that time the search was hopeless. That is the way with opium-smokers. 'Veil after veil must lift' before you recognize reality.

Chapter XIX

THE PURVEYOR OF CHARMS

It was early in 1924, after a visit to U Nyana at the Ma-soe-yin-kyaung-daik, that I first came across the purveyor of Charms. He was not exactly a Buddhist monk, because the Buddhists do not, or should not, believe in charms. However, in olden days such beliefs were widely held, and this old man, a hermit, was one of the few relics of the old tradition. He lived in a bamboo hut outside the monastery wall, and his one room, raised on piles, was enough to thrill any reader of tales about the lost art of black magic. Stuffed lizards hung from the rafters, and on the walls were various reproductions of the Wheel of Life. When I first entered this strange abode, naturally out of curiosity, I found the old sorcerer bent over a pestle and mortar in which he was grinding some reddish-brown liquid. There were the remains of a disembowelled lizard by his side, and as he stirred the mixture he repeated many incantations in a tongue strange to me. I squatted down on the floor and waited for him to finish.

'And what is that, holy one?' I asked. 'Ah!' he said, 'this is a charm against death from a bullet-wound or the thrust of a knife. Would the *thakin* care to try it?' Being at a loose end that afternoon, I decided that I would. I was not, at that time, anticipating any sudden death, but... it would be a new experience. The old man, only distinguishable from the monks by his long hair and long beard, told me to remove my shirt, so that all of the upper part of my body was bare. He then proceeded, with very crude instruments, to inscribe or tattoo certain signs on my body. On my wrists he tattooed three circles; on the points of my shoulder three circles, with their centre dots; on my upper arms he tattooed the figure of a cock, one leg raised, made from the Burmese figures for one to ten; on my chest he tattooed a rough sketch of a pagoda; on the back of my neck three more circles, and on the top of my head something which I could not fathom but which I guessed to be some more circles. The instruments were very primitive, and the process was very painful.

I thought no more of the matter, but a few days later I happened to be in the same neighbourhood and looked in on the old hermit. This time, however, he was not alone. In the corner was seated a man in grey robes whom I knew to be a Chinese priest. The old hermit gave us tea

Chapter XIX : The Purveyor of Charms

and then inquired after my health; I drew back the sleeves of my shirt and showed him the red marks, still slightly inflamed. The Chinese priest was very interested. 'The *thakin* has,' he said, in very good Burmese, 'a charm against death from a knife-thrust or a bullet-wound. These charms are good, but I will give the *thakin* a charm which will protect him from any wound from either knife or gun.'

In a vague sort of way I found this very interesting and inquired what his charm might be. Had I remembered my experiences as a magistrate on the North-east Frontier I might have guessed the form that it would take. He would, he said, write out the charm, and I must attend there every night for thirty-nine nights and, when he had burned the charm, eat the ashes with my rice. Now, I had no objection to eating ashes with my evening rice, but, as I explained to him, it was really impossible for me to attend there every night for thirty-nine nights. He, poor soul, was unaware that every night my presence was required elsewhere. However, the old Chinaman was very insistent. It was a good charm, he said; if I cared to prove it I was welcome to do so. From the wall of the hut he took down a Burmese dah, a keen-bladed sword about two feet in length. As he sat there, cross-legged on the rope-bed, he invited me to cut him anywhere I pleased. I tried the blade on the wooden posts of the bed, and there is no doubt it was razor-sharp, but still I could not bring myself to cut this old man down. After all, I had been a magistrate myself and knew too much about the intricacies of the law. My friend, the old Burmese hermit, however, had no such scruples. He took the dah in his hand and slashed at the thighs of the seated Chinaman. Nothing happened, but, bending forward, I saw that the rough cloth had been cut through, as it were with a pair of scissors, while the flesh underneath showed only a thin red line, as of a scar newly healed.

Even this did not alter my decision. The old Chinaman grew very insistent. Looking deep into my eyes, he said, 'Do as I say or the *thakin* will regret it.' 'And if not?' I asked. 'Then there will follow a great darkness,' he replied, and, try as I would, I could not get him to explain what he meant.

Chapter XX

THE HOUSE OF THE DEER

In a side street, leading off one of the main thoroughfares in the native quarter of Mandalay, lies the House of the Deer. Into this unpretentious house, with the gilded figure of an antlered stag above the doorway, an intermittent stream of Burmese and Chinese may be seen to disappear as dusk falls over the city. They do not enter as folk enter an ordinary dwelling. You will probably see them approaching it with swift, silent steps, maybe yawning prodigiously, and, as you idly watch them, phwt! they are gone. For the House of the Deer is an opium-den, and that swift approach, sudden side-step, and disappearance is the usual way of going into such a place.

The House of the Deer was, as I have said, a very unpretentious den, and there was nothing luxurious about its interior. As you entered you passed, almost directly, into a long room running from front to back, with an L-shaped smoking-platform round two of its sides. At the farther end of this room a doorway leads to a small smoking-room on the right, containing two small platforms in opposite corners, each of which would accommodate a pair of smokers. From this room one door led out into the backyard and another door into another front room, the home of Ah Hpan and his wife.

They were a curiously assorted couple. Ah Hpan was a tall, gaunt, uncouth Chinaman, a hardened smoker and an inveterate gambler. His wife, on the other hand, was short, neat, and plump, impassively serene in her manner, but, as I knew, finding it very difficult, at times, to make both ends meet. It was from observations made during many visits to the House of the Deer that I obtained a certain insight into the manner of running an opium establishment.

The sale of opium in India and Burma is a Government monopoly. Those Asiatics who are habitual opium-smokers or opium-eaters can, under certain conditions, obtain a licence which entitles them to purchase from the Government shops a certain amount of opium each month. The regulations are very strict, and new licences difficult to obtain. The Government, naturally, wishes to prevent the opium habit from spreading, but the powers that be know by experience that it would be unwise and useless to try to cut off the supply of the habitual smoker. They have, therefore, taken the supply into their own hands and, by means of those licences, are endeavouring to eliminate the possibility of a new generation of opium addicts arising.

The scheme, on paper, is very good, and were it water-tight most of the opium-dens would go out of business. However, there are three factors which tend to make this profession of Ah Hpan's profitable, if somewhat hazardous. The first is the resale of opium bought from the Government shops. The second is the smuggling of the drug from outside sources, particularly China; and the third is the corruptibility of certain of the lower ranks of the police.

First of all, therefore, we have the *bona fide* licensed smokers who may, or may not, bring their monthly allowance to Ah Hpan for the necessary preparation before smoking. Naturally, there is no risk attached to this legitimate business and, therefore, very little profit. But among these licensed smokers are a number who do not smoke, or smoke very little. These have, of course, obtained their licences under more or less false pretences, and it is from them that Ah Hpan builds up a stock of opium, good Government opium, for sale to those smokers who cannot obtain a licence.

Smuggling is carried on either by land, across the Chinese frontier, or by sea, into the port of Rangoon. The penalties are severe, but the profits are good. When his stocks were low Ah Hpan absented himself for a while, and journeying to the Shan States, returned with fresh supplies. Many a story I heard from him of men who had been caught. Once the tale was of a white man who had filled the tyres of his car and the spare petrol tin with cake opium, but... someone gave him away. That was the trouble—you never knew in this game who was friend and who spy. Perhaps that was why Ah Hpan never told me how he got his supplies through. But he did tell me one evening, as we smoked together, of a poor woman who was bringing the body of her only child to Mandalay for burial. She had come down with it on a raft from Bhamo, and every one was very sympathetic until, somewhere, someone said something and a subsequent laparotomy by the police revealed a packet of opium where the child's entrails should have been.

Even after the stock of opium has been obtained, legitimately or otherwise, there are the consciences of the local sub-inspector and his policemen to be considered. This is a thorny problem, and Ah Hpan's method of dealing with it was typical of the East. This was a matter about which Ah Hpan would discourse to me very volubly, and once or twice

I saw the process in action. The local police had the power to search any opium-den in order to ensure that no unlicensed smokers were on the premises. If any were found to be there the usual procedure was to remove all the opium-pipes to the police station to be burned. Now, an opium-pipe increases in value the longer it is smoked. The inside of the tube becomes coated and permeated with opium-residue, and there is no smoke like the smoke from an old pipe, especially when musk has been occasionally mixed with the opium. New pipes take a long time to mature, and the police are well aware of this. Consequently, should the proprietor prove ungenerous in his relations with the local sub-inspector, a raid is made and the old pipes removed. The police also know that the proprietor cannot carry on his business without these old-pipes, and that sooner or later he will come to heel. Very probably that same night he will turn up at the station, pay over his arrears, and leave with the bundle of pipes under his arm. In order to make everything appear above board, he will bring with him an equivalent number of new, but valueless, pipes, which will in due course be publicly burned and the fact entered in the station register. Thus are all the proprieties duly observed.

I was present at one such raid at the House of the Deer. That evening I was smoking with Ba Ohn in the little room at the back the premises. Through one of the doors I could see part of the platform in the long room where several couples were smoking in an atmosphere of benignant peace and tranquillity. There also I could see Ah Hpan's wife, in her dark-blue coat and trousers, sitting impassively at the receipt of custom. Through another open doorway I could see Ah Hpan and a Chinese friend playing mah-jong. A third door opened out on to the rear courtyard, and here vision was limited, in the darkness of the night, by a ten-foot bamboo fence which separated the courtyard from the back premises of the other property in the neighbourhood.

Everything was very peaceful, and the only discordant note was struck by a young Burmese railway clerk who was sitting on the opposite platform and talking very volubly to Ba Ohn and myself. His tones were too rapid, too excited, to be mistaken for those of an opium-smoker, and one had only to look at his eyes, his sweat-beaded forehead, and his bubbling lips to realize that here was a cocaine-addict. On the platform by his side was an earth-smeared glass jar with screw top, and it was this that had brought him to me. Some weeks previously a friend of his had gone away on a journey and had buried this jar in his garden to await his return. He had not returned. Someone had whispered something about his errand, and the police had put him away for a spell. Meanwhile his friend had become very curious about the buried pot. The idea gradually grew in his mind that it contained cocaine, and that evening he had dug it up and brought it to the House of the Deer for investigation. It was full of a white powder, but it was not cocaine. Had it been so it would have been worth the best part of a hundred pounds. But no, it was phenacetin or some similar substance such as the illicit drug-vendor is wont to mix in with the genuine cocaine. The man was very disappointed and very angry with his absent friend. Ba Ohn and I listened to his tale and wondered what there was to make a fuss about. The pipe we were smoking was a good one, well scented with musk, and we felt at peace with the world.

Suddenly, without any warning, an amazing thing happened. All those quiet and apparently comatose smokers in the adjacent room rose from their platform, padded swiftly through the room in which I was lying and so out into the night. I heard the splintering of wood and, looking out through the door leading to the courtyard, saw that the bamboo fence was no longer there. It had fallen flat before that stampede of startled humanity. I was at a loss to account for this sudden exodus until, turning my gaze back to the room, I saw smiling down on me a sub-inspector of police. Behind him stood Ah Hpan, evidently in a great state of nervous agitation. Ba Ohn, however, who had once been a clerk in a Government office, knew all about sub-inspectors and scarcely gave him a glance. He went on preparing the next pellet and signed to me to lie down.

The inspector, indeed, proved to be a very affable gentleman. Ah Hpan had, apparently, been a little behindhand with his payments, but all that was now settled. We exchanged a few pleasantries, and he bowed himself out, instructing Ah Hpan, as he went, to see that we were not disturbed. What amazed me more than the complacency of the police was the panic of the opium-smokers. It seemed to me inconceivable that any *habitué* of an opium-den could, while smoking, be able to collect his wits together quickly enough to make such a rapid get-away. It was not till I had reflected that these men were unlicensed, and that had they been caught and detained their source of supply would be automatically cut off, that I realized that it was not terror of the police that had lent wings to their feet but something far more terrible, a foretaste of which I had myself experienced in those dimly lit halls of the Ma-soe-yin-kyaung-daik.

This little episode raised me greatly in the esteem of Ah Hpan, who, as a general rule, had little use for foreign devils. He seemed to think that while I was there as one of his customers the House of the Deer would be safe from police interference. When his little baby daughter was born his cup of happiness appeared to be full. Like most Chinese, he was an affectionate father, and night after night I would watch him walking up and down along the line of incurious smokers, addressing the tiny bundle in his arms as 'little bitch' in order to ward off the evil eye. But even this scrupulous care in his choice of epithets did not save the child, and her death after a few weeks led to the only trouble that I had in that house.

I had been spending the day with a wealthy old Chinese friend of mine in his secluded little bungalow, surrounded by trees and tucked away in the heart of the city. Such places always fascinated me. They were so cool and quiet, the servants so attentive but unobtrusive, that it was difficult to realize that a few hundred yards away was the bustle and roar of the main streets of the bazaar. In the morning the old man had taken me to see one of the Chinese temples, a walled enclosure with a central shrine and many fearsome coloured images. After a light and excellent tiffin which, I am glad to say, did not contain any of those horrible dishes about which I had heard so much, we adjourned to my old friend's private room for a smoke and a chat. The room was attractive in its simplicity. A low, broad, lacquered couch, one exquisite scroll-painting, a vase of flowers, and a hideously beautiful joss made up the sum total of the furnishings. There were no carpets, no velvet curtains, and no softly shaded lights, as in my own smoking-room, and I realized that, whereas this room was strictly utilitarian and nevertheless visually satisfying, my room was merely a bizarre innovation furnished with the mundane prodigality of a *parvenu*. The pipes were extraordinarily beautiful, being of carved ivory, silver, and jade, but, sweet as they were, I could not but endorse the common sentiment among smokers that a well-matured bamboo pipe is hard to beat. The pellets were prepared by a silent, impassive serving-man who manipulated them dexterously over a lamp, the glass shade of which was gay with charming little paintings of Chinese workmanship. It was all very pleasant, and the tea which we sipped from the tiny cups was scented and of the best.

Towards evening, however, we heard a slight commotion out in the compound, and a young Zerbadi, Ba Maung, was shown in. I knew him well as he had often shared my pipe at the House of the Deer. He was young, a trifle darker than the pure-bred Burman, and I had often noticed him, as we smoked, casting his lustful dark eyes in the direction of Ah Hpan's wife. This had interested me because, as a rule, when the little lamps are lit, women are pushed strictly into the background of an opium-smoker's mind. Not that he is averse to them or is incapable of enjoying their company. In fact, the Burmese have a saying which means that a woman loves a man who smokes opium. The reason for this apparently

Chapter XX : The House of the Deer   85

strange statement lies in the effect of opium on the nervous system. Even as it slows down the reception of sight, sounds, and ideas, so that their true import takes a comparatively long time to reach the brain, so does the drug introduce into intercourse between the sexes that dalliance which is reminiscent of the early days of courtship. However, let me return to Ba Maung and his news.

It appeared from his rather incoherent account that Ah Hpan had returned that morning from one of his periodical visits to the Shan States, where he had presumably gone to renew his supplies of opium. While he was there awaiting the arrival of his agent, he had passed the time in gambling and had lost a certain amount of money. His wife on learning of this had upbraided him, and, the nerves of both being on edge after the loss of their child, matters seemed to be nearing a crisis. The other *habitués* of the den, worried at this disturbance in their midst and fearing the worst, had sent Ba Maung to fetch me, as it was known that I was one of the few men for whom Ah Hpan had any respect.

My own feelings towards Ah Hpan had never been sympathetic. He lacked that suave and gentle courtesy which was the hall-mark of most of my Chinese acquaintances, but his wife had always been very good to me, bringing me occasional bowls of soup in which floated tough, rubbery sea-leeches. I also knew that they were, in reality, very fond of each other, and I decided that I had better go, lest he should unwittingly do her some grievous harm for which he would later be extremely sorry. Accordingly I made my excuses to my host and, with Ba Maung, hurried off to the House of the Deer.

As I passed through the long smoking-room I saw Ah Hpan, his face flushed, smoking by himself. On the tray, in addition to the lamp and other paraphernalia, was a bottle of very fiery spirits. This did not look too good, but, taking no notice, we passed into the little back room and settled down on our usual platform.

As the neatly dressed, impassive little woman brought us a tiny cup of opium from the front room, Ah Hpan caught sight of her through the open doorway and let forth a volley of abuse. My knowledge of Chinese is very slight and mainly confined to the swear-words used by Chinese muleteers, but I knew enough to realize that his would have made even a mule kick. It was enough, indeed, to ruffle even the impassivity of Ah Hpan's wife, and she proceeded forthwith to have hysterics. I lifted her up in my arms, declining the rather over-eager proffers of help from hot-blooded Ba Maung, and carried her into the front room, where I laid her on the floor. Her little heels beat a violent tattoo on the rush matting, while from her usually immobile lips poured out a stream of high-pitched and colourful epithets. I tried to quieten her, but it was of no avail, so I went back to my pipe. The shrill wail of her voice and the beating of her heels were still shattering the usual peace of the House of the Deer when a shout from a smoker in the long room caused me to look up. In the doorway stood Ah Hpan, his eyes ablaze and an evil-looking knife in his hand. It is a curious and unusual thing to see a Chinaman flush red, and it is also a curious and very unusual thing for an opium-smoker to drink alcohol while he smokes. Anyway, he made a very unpleasant spectacle as he stood there swaying in the doorway.

Fortunately for all concerned, the hectic events of the evening had had the effect of keeping my brain clear; otherwise, had I been in the usual state induced by opium-smoking, I might well have watched Ah Hpan kill his wife without being aware of the import of the action until it was too late. As it was I was able to get up and, closing the door leading into the front room, I stood with my back against it.

Now, in those days, under normal circumstances, I was as much afraid of death as any man, but, here, the circumstances were not normal. At the back of the mind of every smoker of opium is a fear that is more terrible than the fear of death. I have watched opium-smokers die of the plague—not many of them, as the drug appears to afford a certain immunity—and I can vouch for the fact that they died unafraid so long as their bellies were full of smoke. It was, therefore, with a rather detached feeling of curiosity that I watched the crouching figure of Ah Hpan sidle over the floor towards where I stood. There was madness born of rank alcohol and opium in his eyes, and from his long, lean throat came a low, guttural stream of filthy abuse. And then I hit him, straight between those bloodshot eyes, and he went down like a log, the knife falling from his hand and clattering to the floor. We picked him up and laid him on the platform in the long room, tying his hands and feet against the time when he should recover consciousness. I returned to my smoke with Ba Maung and was surprised to find that my pulse-beats were as regular as ever.

When I called at the House of the Deer the next evening Ah Hpan himself welcomed me and, in his uncouth, abrupt fashion, thanked me for what I had done the night before, while his little wife, smooth, neat, and placid as usual, brought me an extra tasty bowl of soup with an extra large and rubbery sea-leech floating on top.

Chapter XXI

A NIGHT IN THE JUNGLE AND A DECISION

The year had turned full circle, and the cold weather of 1923-24 was nearing its close when an incident occurred which caused me once more to take stock of my position. The Poet, another man, and I had motored out to a village in the foot-hills of the jungle-covered range of mountains which rise some forty miles to the east of Mandalay. The Poet was hardly one's idea of a mighty hunter before the Lord. Pale and delicate in appearance, but otherwise healthy enough, he looked what he was—a poet. But poets, like woman with child, have peculiar fancies, and this one wanted to shoot an elephant. I could never understand why, unless it was to demonstrate to what extent God had given to man, even to a poet, dominion over the beasts of the field. Neither the friend nor I had any such blood-lust, but we felt that the sight might be interesting.

On arriving at the village trackers were engaged, and the Poet made ready to set out. His friend had decided to stay in camp, but I agreed to accompany the party to take photographs at the scene of massacre. Perhaps I too might shoot an elephant. Bad shot though I knew myself to be, I felt sure that I could hardly miss an elephant, provided that I was within close enough range. I had hardly gone half a mile when my enthusiasm waned, and I decided not to break the First Precept, but to allow my elephant to go free. The head tracker did not, however, like the idea of my returning to camp; it was unlucky, he said. Some misfortune would overtake the party. But I was not in a mood to heed these superstitions and went back to join the third member of the expedition among the cold chicken and bottled beer.

The day passed pleasantly enough, but as the afternoon drew on and there was no sign of the hunters' return I began to grow a little anxious. My anxiety was not on behalf of the Poet. The Burmese elephants, so the villagers assured us, were such accommodating animals that if not in a suitable position to be shot they would move round in response to a smack on their hind-parts from one of the beaters. No, it was the knowledge that the time was rapidly approaching when they would be trimming the little lamps down in the opium-dens that was the cause of my concern. I had made arrangements so that I should be back by six o'clock... and I did not want to be caught napping.

It was well past five when we caught sight of the slight figure of the Poet running towards us. It was evident that something had gone wrong, so we hurried to meet him. In a state of great agitation he told us of the tragedy which had befallen the expedition. They had followed the spoor of several elephants and had eventually come up with a herd feeding in the jungle. He had been standing, his heavy rifle cocked, waiting for a bull to turn, when the head tracker, who was standing beside him, noticed a wild buffalo emerging from a near-by thicket. He had put out his hand to draw the attention of the Poet to this new danger, and the rifle had gone off, the heavy bullet entering the old man's left thigh and, as I could well understand, making a ghastly mess of his leg. The Poet, as might have been expected, was not very good in a crisis. He had left the man there with the rest of the party and, accompanied by one guide, had returned to camp as speedily as possible.

A hurried discussion followed, and it was decided that one of us should return with the guide and some of the villagers to bring in the wounded man, while the other two drove into Mandalay to fetch a surgeon. The Poet was too exhausted to think of doing the return trip, and the other man was not over-keen, so the lot fell on me. This was, of course, only natural, as I was the only member of the party who had an intimate acquaintance with jungles, and, after all, had I not been the one who, by turning back, had brought this misfortune on the expedition? So, slinging a revolver over my shoulder, I set out with three or four villagers and my guide. I had hardly passed out of sight of the camp and entered the jungle when my face parted in a cheek-splitting yawn. I glanced at my wrist-watch; it was six o'clock exactly. They would be lighting the lamps in the House of the Deer. I had very nearly been caught napping; yes, very nearly, but not quite, as I had in my pocket a little tin box full of pellets of cooked opium, my inseparable companions. They would at least serve to stave off the terror until I could get back to my own pipes. I slipped one into my mouth and set off again at a jog-trot.

That was a nightmare of a journey. We had not gone very far when darkness fell upon us. We collected dry wood and made torches, but it was soon evident that our task was going to be no easy one. Our guide, who doubtless could have found his way back by daylight, got hopelessly lost. For hours we wandered up and down the jungle-covered hillsides, stopping every now and then to send out a call and listening intently but in vain for a reply. It was an eerie experience. The tall trees on either side

Chapter XXI : A Night in the Jungle and a Decision

of the narrow game tracks looked like the aisles of some lofty cathedral as they were illumined by the flickering light of our torches. The night-hunting beasts of the forest gave us a wide berth, and, truth to tell, we heeded them little, so great was our haste and so urgent our need.

It was midnight before we heard at last a faint response to our shouts, and very soon afterwards we came upon the party, squatting round a fire. The wounded man was lying near by, and a brief examination showed that his leg from the thigh downward was indeed in a ghastly mess. No one had done anything to it, and it was surprising that the man had not bled to death. Removing the lanyard from the revolver, I fixed a tourniquet at the top of the thigh and gave the man a couple of opium pellets. We then set about cutting down bamboo and branches to make a stretcher. This completed, we prepared to make the best of our way back to camp.

If the journey out had been trying the return was infinitely more so. It was bitterly cold, and we could only move slowly. Every half-hour or so we would halt and kindle a big fire by which to warm our chilled bodies. No one knew the way, but every now and again the old tracker would recover consciousness and, looking up at the stars, would indicate the main direction which we had to follow. It was a very cold, tired, and depressed party which stumbled into camp about 6.30 the next morning. Here were cars, a surgeon, and hot drinks. As the sun rose I set off for Mandalay, arriving about nine o'clock. Ba Ohn was waiting for me; he had been there all night. I stretched myself out luxuriously on the soft-carpeted platform while he prepared the pipe. I had smoked hardly more than three or four pills when my tired muscles and nerves relaxed and I slept, my head still on the little, raised smoking-pillow, and did not wake until midnight.

During those long hours in the jungle my mind had been very active. I knew that had I not had those pellets with me, I should have been in a very bad way. And once again it seemed to me that I must endeavour to break away before it was too late. I thought of the plans which I had made a year previously, when I had returned to Mandalay from the North-east Frontier, of those gold deposits of which I knew in the Ahkyang Valley. I had taken those nuggets down to Rangoon and had had them examined by a very well-known English mineralogist attached to the Rangoon University. This expert had been very impressed and had given me a letter to one of the trading firms in Rangoon, by whom he was retained in an advisory capacity. I had shown the nuggets and the report to the Rangoon manager of this firm, but he would have nothing to do with my schemes. But he thought enough about the prospects to refuse to allow me to retain the expert's report, which, as he stated, was addressed to him.

Then, towards the end of the year, I had sent out a small expedition to the Ahkyang to trade and to bring back further specimen nuggets. I had placed in charge of it a young Kachin whom I could trust. This was the very same lad whose head I had clouted in that Lisu village when I decided that life on the Frontier was getting a little too much for me. I had heard nothing further of the expedition, but it was more than likely that they would not be able to return till the spring of 1925. I should have gone myself, but by that time I was no longer free.

Meanwhile during these past twelve months I had endeavoured in a desultory way to run a motor-hire business, but it had not been successful. I was no business-man, and my thoughts were elsewhere.

Yes, it had been a wasted year, a terrible year, but a very interesting year. If it were not to have a tragic ending, however, I must break away from this slavery. My free passage to England was still available if I took it before June. It might be my last chance, my last opportunity. I would return to England for a few months and see if I could raise any interest there in these gold deposits.

And it was with thoughts such as these that I had sat, chilled to the bone, by those camp-fires in the jungle that night. I knew that the matter would not be easy, but I did not feel that the break would be impossible if I went the right way about it. A day or two later I enlisted the help of the ancients and moderns; I went first to see an Army doctor and then down to the little hut where lived my friend the hermit, the purveyor of charms.

Chapter XXII

THE LAST CHANCE

The moderns, in the person of a Burmese Army doctor, gave my problem long and careful consideration. He was no fool and could appreciate the difficulty of my position. He realized that the chains must be broken gradually. He knew, as far as the uninitiated can know, the terrors through which I should have to pass, and he was prepared to offer me a temporary relief should those terrors prove intolerable. In effect, he gave me, on condition that I should carry out my plan, a prescription for a hypodermic syringe and morphia to be taken only when I felt that the need was urgent. I knew all that there was to be known about morphia, even from that day in 1916 in Mandalay, when, suffering from excruciating tooth-ache, I had been injected by the regimental doctor and had found a sublime release from pain. I had seen also men who, in the effort to escape from the bonds of opium, had taken to morphia, and I had seen their bodies, the legs and arms punctured with the tiny pin-pricks. But to me, in the state that I was, it seemed a refuge, a last line of defence in the battle which I was waging.

The old hermit in the little hut at the gates of the monastery heard my tale with as much interest but less sympathy. Yes, he said, he could give me something which would exorcize the devils which beset me. I turned my head away as he began chanting his weird mantras and mixing obscene things in his bowl. The resulting concoction, which I was to drink each night when the call of the little lamps came upon me, was the most revolting mixture it has ever been my misfortune to taste.

Armed with these safeguards, I took the train for Rangoon, where I put up at the house of the Poet, pending the departure of the boat for England. On the night of my arrival things were bad. Towards evening the old call came, and I was in sore straits. The Poet's aunt, a lady whom I dearly loved, gave me an injection of morphia, but something must have gone wrong, for I fainted and then was very sick. The next night I felt that I could not risk a recurrence of this incident, and I took a rickshaw down to the Chinese quarter of Rangoon.

I knew nothing about the opium-dens in this city, but it was not long before I found myself in one of them. The lay-out was totally different from those in Mandalay. Instead of one long, low platform, there were ranged alongside the walls tier upon tier of bunks, each holding a pair of smokers. I ordered my opium, settled myself in one of the lower bunks and started to smoke. I was alone, but by this time was perfectly capable of preparing my own pills. As I smoked I looked upward to the tier of bunks on the other side of the long, narrow room. Suspicious glances were being cast at me from the slitted eyes of the Chinese there. There was trouble brewing. I had been accepted in every den in Mandalay, but here I was a stranger and, they surmised, a police spy. A low murmur grew round the room. A man slid down from an upper bunk and approached me in a threatening manner. I rose to my feet, and immediately the place was in an uproar. From bunks on either side they sprang down, these almond-eyed, yellow-faced Chinese, and came for me with knife and pipe. The proprietor and I fought our way, inch by inch, back through the room to a door in the rear, where I turned tail and fled.

The next day I boarded the steamer that was to take me home to those primroses and violets about which I had dreamed—it seemed so many, many years ago. The plan which I had arranged with the aid of my friends and the Army doctor was to report to the ship's doctor, and to place all the facts in his hands. Ships' doctors, they all informed me, were the salt of the earth and would never let me down. I found the doctor sitting in the lee of his cabin, reading a book. He was young, supercilious, and, as soon as I cast my eyes on him, I knew that I had drawn a blank. However, I went through with it. Without even rising from his deck-chair and hardly raising his eyes from his book, he listened to my story. He then asked what drugs I had brought on board. I showed him the hypodermic syringe, the morphia tablets, some opium pellets, and a few small green tissue packets containing cocaine. He took them and, without a word, threw them overboard.

It is some five days from Rangoon to Colombo, and during those five days I never slept. I haunted the door of the doctor's cabin, and as I watched this fresh-faced young man dressing for dinner I cursed him from the depths of my tormented soul. In those days I had some semblance of a belief in a personal God, and it had been one of my comforting reflections that when finally God took me by the ear and said, 'Well, my son, what kind of mess have you made of your life?' I could reply that at least I bore no ill-will towards any man. But this young doctor, so clever and so attractive to the ladies on board, filled my soul with hatred. I had trusted him, and he had betrayed my trust; I would never trust him again.

Chapter XXII : The Last Chance

It is easy enough for me to recall the past, but even now, after a lapse of so many years, I prefer to leave a veil over those five days. Suffice it to say that the Terror seized hold of me and rent me, body and soul. Night after night I sat on my heels by the door of the doctor's cabin until, irritated by my importunity, he would throw me a small opium pill from his medicine chest. For a brief hour or two I would find relief, but it was not enough, it was not enough. The bonds were not to be broken as easily as that.

When the ship reached Colombo I went ashore, and the same evening I sat in a little tea-shop waiting for the subordinate Government officials to return from work. They passed by, very different from the gaily clothed Burmese whom I knew so well. But I was waiting for something which I knew to be common to all, whatever their outward appearance. Soon I found it, a young Cingalee yawning fit to burst his head off. I rose and followed. It was a long trail, through the outskirts of the city, up a by-path into the jungle, and it finally ended at a miserable hut in a clearing. But I knew what I should find there.

When I returned to the ship late that night I had smoked myself back to contentment, and in my pocket I had a box with a plentiful supply of pills. I did not trouble the young doctor that night, and the next day, when I met his supercilious smile in the dining-saloon, I knew that he knew that he had failed, and also that he did not care. How I hated that man! He had had the chance; I had given myself into his hands, trusted him, and the fool had failed me because his early won F.R.C.S. had given him ideas of his knowledge of life, whereas in reality he knew less about the world than any old G.P. who had drunk his way through the Seven Seas in God knows what forsaken old cargo-boats.

At Port Said I renewed my stocks of drugs. During our brief stay I found my way to an obscene house where I was able to obtain a ball of raw opium and some cocaine. The offer of the obsequious proprietor to throw in other services was declined.

Leaving this building at length with my two precious packages, I retraced my steps through the narrow alley-ways to the ship. The whole transaction had been carried out with smoothness and expedition, and it was well that it had happened so, for the need was urgent. The ship was only staying in the port a few hours, and but for my knowledge of opium and the habits of its addicts the whole business would have been impossible. I met the doctor as I reached the head of the gangway, and, though we exchanged no word, I was sure that he knew on what errand I had been ashore, and, not being utterly a fool, he could tell from the look on my face that I had been successful.

I was at this time occupying the hospital cabin in the after-part of the ship. This isolation had been rendered necessary by the complaints of my fellow-passenger in the cabin amidships. Although I was totally unaware of the fact, it appeared that I raved and cursed in my sleep throughout the night, and it was not unnatural that my companion found it somewhat trying. There were, it is true, two dreams which began at that time to haunt me in my sleep. In the first I found myself climbing a mountain, the grass-covered slopes of which were so steep that I had to proceed on hands and knees. I have no head for heights, and I was afraid to look down, but I knew that the slope by which I had ascended was long and precipitous. When within a few feet of the summit, the goal of my desire, I felt myself slipping, and then I would awake in a sweat of terror. The second dream was equally terrifying. I was standing in the trench of a perimeter camp on the North-west Frontier, and a host of fanatical tribesmen were rushing to the attack. I raised my revolver to fire at the foremost man, and as I pulled the trigger I saw the bullet slowly leave the barrel, describe a gentle curve, and strike harmlessly against the man's breast. Yes, they were not pleasant dreams, but very suggestive.

As the ship steamed through the Mediterranean I recalled the time, nine years previously, when I had made my first voyage across that sea. Gibraltar, Malta, and Port Said had seemed wonderful places to me then. True, the villainous guides had been careful to show us the sights which they apparently thought would prove the most attractive to a civilized young Englishman. We had found such experiences interesting, but they had left little impression on our young souls, from which the cellophane wrappings had hardly been removed.

But now I was returning morally degenerate; not on account of any of the lusts of the flesh to which man is heir (such, at least, would have been normal and might have been excusable), but because I had, out of curiosity, poked my head into a web as intangible as smoke, but stronger than any fetters forged by human hands.

I experienced no thrill as we sighted the patchwork of little fields on the hills behind Plymouth. The thought of primroses and violets in the Surrey woods, which had been so pleasant a year before, failed to move me. I knew that I was playing a losing game, and that, when I had cut that ship's doctor as partner, I might as well have thrown my hand in.

Chapter XXIII

THE RETURN

Those three hot summer months in England brought no relief to my soul or body. The clear, clean landscapes of the Yorkshire moors and Cornish coast only served to accentuate the abyss into which I felt myself slipping. As I lay on the cliffs and gazed out over the Bristol Channel my eyes were only for the ships, outward bound, maybe, for the East. The ball of opium which I had obtained at Port Said grew daily smaller and smaller, and I watched its gradual diminution with growing anxiety. I knew that I should have to go back. The spell was too strong. Very subtly it had woven itself about me during the previous year, slowly sapping my mental virility until at last I had given up the struggle. I would stay, I thought, until the opium was nearly finished, and then I would return and never come back.

And then a terrible thing happened. I was staying with an old school friend on a farm on the Yorkshire moors. One morning, while playing tennis with his sisters, I lost the little ball of opium. I had always carried it about with me, and it must have fallen from my pocket during the game. All round the court and among the flower-beds I searched, much to the amazement of my friends, who thought that I was making rather an unnecessary amount of fuss about the loss of a pill. But they did not know what it was and what it meant to me. I enlisted the help of a little boy in my search, and he entered into this game of treasure-hunting with great gusto, little realizing how much more than the proffered reward of half-a-crown I would have gladly given him if he could have found it.

But there was no sign of it, and in a sweat of terror I got out my car and drove into Scarborough. I felt that it was better that I should be alone in this crisis. I booked a room at a small hotel and, having had a bottle of whisky sent up, locked the door and sat down to wait. At about six o'clock I began to feel what I can only describe as an uneasiness in my thighs, and I knew that it was coming.

I awoke next morning, still sitting in the chair, with the empty bottle on the table by my side. I was feeling pretty rotten, of course, but the spirits had done the trick. Nevertheless, I knew that I could not go on drinking whisky like that. If I had to come to a sticky end, I thought it had better be through opium than through drink. I had seen devotees of both cults, and I preferred the benignant abstractions of the opium-smoker to the beastliness of the confirmed drunkard. The path of the smoker, as long as he had his smoke, was a primrose path, and, unlike the drunkard, his addiction was a matter that affected only himself.

By chance my plans were practically completed for my return to Burma, and my passage had been booked. But these intervening days before I sailed were not very pleasant ones. It was with a feeling of relief, and in the certain knowledge that I should never return, that I boarded the steamer at Liverpool. My plans to form a company to exploit the gold in the Ahkyang Valley had failed, but I had with me a sufficiency of funds, subscribed by relations, to enable me to carry on till the return of the little expedition which I had fitted out the year before. It was a gamble, of course; but there was always the possibility that there might be news of the Kachin and his mule caravan before the end of the cold weather. That the gold was there I knew, and although the nuggets had been stolen during my stay in Mandalay, several of my friends, including one of my brothers, had seen them when first I returned from the North-east Frontier. The question was, however, whether I could last out until the arrival of such news. It was now October 1924, and I knew that the roads up to the frontier would be passable for mules until after April. This left about six months, and during that time, in my present condition anything might happen. If I could only get hold of some further nuggets, I thought, and forward them, with my maps, to the proper quarter I should be content to leave any further exploitation to others more competent than I.

As for myself, I had no illusions about my future and ultimate destiny. I was returning, a willing captive, to captivity, the taste of temporary freedom bitter in my mouth. And so, night after night, as we ploughed our way through the Bay and the Mediterranean I drank myself into a stupor, aching and longing for the time when all my fears and anxieties would be wafted away in the fumes of forgetfulness. My attempts at escape had been futile, like those dream bullets describing gentle curves and falling harmlessly on the breasts of the advancing tribesmen. Below me lay that dream abyss, but I was tired of struggling up the mountain-side to that unattainable summit, and now was prepared to let go and fall and fall and fall.

On arrival at Port Said I hurried ashore and sought out my smiling Egyptian from whom I had obtained the opium. He welcomed me with open arms, and for a long time we sat in the cool upper room, sipping coffee and discussing business. Yes, said the Egyptian, he could get me some opium and some cocaine, if I wanted it, but—at a price. He eyed me keenly from under his long lashes, estimating the urgency of my need. I fear that it was only too apparent, and the signs were evidently familiar to him. I was in no condition to haggle, and the bargain was soon clinched.

He rose and left the room, returning a few minutes later with a packet of cocaine and a ball of opium. Restraining my eagerness with an effort, I cut off a portion, rolled it into a pill, and swallowed it, washing it down with a gulp of the sweet, strong coffee. I then sat back on the divan waiting, a smile of anticipatory pleasure twitching about the corners of my mouth. In a little while it came—the relief, the relaxation of tension. Not as great as one gets from the smoking, but ineffably blissful after the restless torment of the past weeks. The Egyptian sat watching me, smiling. I smiled back and, for the first time, looked on him with a kindly tolerance. I felt at peace with the world again.

As the drug continued its work I leaned back luxuriously and laughed aloud. Then I began to question the red-fezzed figure by my side as to the Port Said smoking-dens. No, he said, he knew of no opium-dens, but if I liked he could take me to a place where they smoked hashish. I knew nothing about hashish except that it was made from hemp, but I thought that the experience would be interesting, and as the boat did not leave till the next day I decided to go.

I followed my guide through a maze of narrow alleys until he eventually came to rest outside a door let into a mud wall. The usual knock or call, followed by an exchange of whispers, which I have always associated with such places, followed. The proceeding never fails to send a thrill of excitement down my spine. The door opened, and we ascended a dark flight of stairs into a small room. It was ill-lit, dusty, and dirty. Round three of the walls were benches, and on these sat the most villainous collection of humanity it has ever been my lot to meet. In the middle of the floor was an enormous water-pipe, similar to the hookahs which I had known in India. This pipe was being passed from man to man, and the stem, or mouthpiece, was of such a length that there was no need to shift the main body of the pipe. This merely pivoted in the centre of the floor while the mouthpiece traversed the circle of guests. There was hardly any talking as the pipe passed round and round, the bowl in the centre being replenished from time to time by an ancient acolyte. It was a weird spectacle, so vastly different from the refinement, cleanliness, and comfort of the opium-dens of the East. I took my turn at the pipe with the rest and found the smoke a good deal more acrid than that of opium. I had plenty of time, however, to observe this strange assembly of cut-throats—Arabs, Bedouin, and Egyptians—wild-eyed and silent. They were a tough lot.

It was close on midnight before my guide and I slipped out through the little door into the street. I had been so interested in the comings and goings of this queer company that I had not noticed the passage of time or how much hashish I was smoking. I felt very grateful for the presence of my friend as we passed through those dark lanes and byways. Slit throats and rifled bodies did not seem out of place in those surroundings and in that company. I returned to the ship, well pleased and excited at the events of the day, and that night I slept fathoms deep.

Chapter XXIV

THE ABYSS

It was before dawn on a morning in November when I stepped out of my deck-cabin to witness once again the magic of sunrise over the Irrawaddy Delta. Above the mist-covered sandbanks rose the *hti*s of little white pagodas, but it was for the sight of the first rays of the sun on the golden *hti* of the Shwe Dagon Pagoda that I waited. This was my welcome back to Burma, the land of my adoption, the land that had known and was to know the extremes of my joy and my tragedy. I yearned for her as a soul yearns for reunion with the infinite, and yet with that yearning was a sadness, a poignancy as if of farewell.

The voyage from Port Said had been uneventful. The renewal of my supply of opium had lessened my desire for drink. At Colombo I had revisited the little hut in the jungle and replenished my supplies. And these had been pills of cooked opium, a vast improvement on the raw product which I had obtained at the House of Perversion.

Burma! Ye gods, how I loved this land and its people. If there were anything stronger than my soul-surrender to opium it was not my submission to any faith, my hope for any hereafter, but my love for this land of tolerance and gaiety, of silks and saffron. People of the West might desire to pass away in the company of their loved ones, but here in Burma I felt that, however lonely might be my passing, my soul would be happy in the company of many unknown but lovable fellow-pilgrims on The Way.

Rangoon was looking its old self as we approached our moorings. It was with a feeling of returning home that I took a taxi and drove up the main street past the Sule Pagoda to the hotel in the Cantonments where I had decided to spend the night. The atmosphere of the place, the sights, the sounds, and the smells filled me with a content which cannot be described.

That evening I entertained several of the ship's officers to dinner, and after they had gone I sat in my room musing on the voyage and my exultation at being back again in Burma. Then a visitor was announced, and there appeared before me a young Burman dressed in the height of fashion—blue coat, gorgeous silk skirt, silk head-dress, and the whole *ensemble* glittering with diamonds. Astonished as I was by this display of wealth, a glance at the man's eyes was sufficient to identify him. This man was the proprietor of the house in which I had lived so long in the Shoemakers' Quarter at Mandalay. He was the offspring of a Sino-Burmese union, and his comical face and flickering eyelids had always been to me a source of amusement. His wife, I remembered, had lived on the ground floor of my house, and had been an extremely attractive woman. The husband had had what, as I have mentioned before, the Burmese term a private wife. However, this had not prevented him from being jealous of me, and one night he had sat up behind the water-butt till dawn waiting for me, a sword in his hand and murder in his heart. During that time I had entered the house by a back entrance, and all unwitting of the lurking danger outside the front door, had been exchanging sweet nothings with the lady within.

Before I had left Burma, however, I had obtained for this lad, whom I really liked, a post as Sub-Inspector in the Police. I was therefore surprised to see him in a state of such apparent opulence. He accepted my offer of a drink, and we began to talk. At first the conversation took the usual course of inquiries about mutual acquaintances and my visit to England and the Wembley Exhibition. But as the whisky in the bottle diminished, so did his expansiveness increase. Police work, he said, was no good. There was a certain amount of money to be made from it, it was true, but not enough. He knew of a better way. Would I come in it with him? I poured him out another whisky and asked for further details. Well, he said, there were ways and means of manufacturing hundred-rupee notes. One went to Japan and learned the technique, and then one returned to Rangoon, where at certain Japanese shops watermarked paper could be obtained. It was all very easy. Then one could buy diamond buttons for one's engyo and keep one's private wife in the state which she deserved. It was all so easy... so much easier than police work... so much easier... would not the *thakin* join in? He then fell asleep on the floor of my room, and as I wrapped a blanket about him I felt very kindly towards this child of the East who had been so eager to share his good fortune with me. Neither the pure gold of the Ahkyang Valley nor the forged notes of Rangoon could seduce me from my allegiance to the White Poppy, and the next day I left for Mandalay.

Little Ba Set, neat and clean in his blue jacket and silk *lungyi*, was waiting on the platform to welcome me as the train steamed into Mandalay station. His honest, ugly little face was wreathed in smiles as he bowed before me, and from under the long lashes of his slit-like eyes I caught an expression which made me suddenly lift the little figure up to hold him close. He worshipped me, that boy, and the thought of it made me feel

4. *Little Ba Set, The Ever-Faithful.*

terribly humble and unworthy and grateful. We left the station and drove down together to the little wooden house in the Shoemakers' Quarter, where he lived with his widowed mother. They insisted on my staying there while I looked about for a house, the one which I had previously rented now being occupied. The little house was as neat and clean as Ba Set, and I was glad to avail myself of the offer.

Outside in the streets the sound of music and singing proclaimed that this was a night of festival. Inside we sat round a low table and ate our evening meal of curry and rice. It was good to be back again, whatever happened. As the dusk fell fairy lights and paper lanterns began to gleam in and around the houses and their compounds. On the other side of the road a *pwe* was in progress, the shrill voices of the dancing-girls and the twanging of the instruments rising clear above the laughter and chatter of the gaily dressed crowd. Yes, it was good to be back, but I must have news, and I knew that there was only one place where I should find it. So I left my kindly hostess and Ba Set, and, telling them that I should return later, slipped away to the House of the Deer.

A murmur of surprise and soft greetings rose from the recumbent forms of the smokers as I made my way through the long room. Ah Hpan, at the farther end, raised himself on one elbow, and his harsh, uncouth words of welcome jarred discordantly on that otherwise harmonious scene. His little wife rose from her desk, and an almost imperceptible smile flickered across her impassive features as she hurried out to the back of the house, there to prepare, I felt sure, an extra delicately flavoured bowl of sea-leech soup. In the inner room I found Ba Ohn.

He was smoking alone, and in the light of the little oil-lamp looked as decoratively beautiful as ever. He had evidently been expecting me, for, hardly raising his eyes from the pill he was preparing, he motioned me to the vacant place on the other side of the tray with a wave of the long pipe. As we smoked I knew that he was studying me from under his long lashes, but no word passed between us until the languor of body and mind told me that I was in a suitable condition to receive any news, however bad, abstractedly. Well for me that it was so; for there was no news of the little mule caravan and my most trusted assistant had absconded with my sole remaining motor-car, on the hire proceeds of which I had been depending to carry me over the next three or four months. I smoked long into the night, and as the hours passed my troubles fell away from me, and I thought only of how pleasant it was to be in the company of Ba Ohn again and to watch those slim, deft hands manipulating the nipple-like pellets in the glow of the little oil-lamp.

Chapter XXIV : The Abyss

The next day I rented a house in the Jewellers' Quarter overlooking a main thoroughfare into which ran the street where Ba Set and his mother lived. The house was two-storeyed and on a plan similar to that of the one I had occupied in the Shoemakers' Quarter, except that access to the upper storey was not obtained through a trap-door, but by means of an outside staircase at the back of the house. My servants occupied the ground floor while I lived upstairs. The lay-out of the large room was identical with that of my former residence, even to the smoking-room and small niche in the wall where reposed my little statue of Buddha, this flanked by two vases of Burmese silver filled with pagoda blossoms. The incongruity of these two furnishings, in view of the Buddha's Fifth Precept against the taking of strong drink and drugs, had always been apparent to me but not inconsistent with my philosophy. True, I was not a good Buddhist, but it was not for want of trying. An effort to escape from The Wheel, even if it fails, is worthy of merit. I had struggled desperately, but the odds had been too heavy against me, and I was now prepared to let go, believing that in the strivings of the body lie the tempering of the spirit, but too worn out and sapped of willpower to struggle any more.

The fall, with its inevitable acceleration, was rapid enough in all conscience. Before my departure for England I had confined my smoking, as a rule, to the evenings; but now, as the year of 1924 approached its end, I began to smoke in the mornings and then in the afternoons, until finally the sessions aggregated some twelve hours a day. In the morning I smoked in my own apartment from eight o'clock to eleven and continued in the afternoon, after a light lunch, from two until five. Soon after six o'clock I would go down to the House of the Deer or some other opium-den and there smoke, mainly in the company of Ba Ohn, until after midnight. Here I would lie, listening to the discreetly whispered gossip of the city and waiting for any news from up country.

I saw very little of my friends during these days, and, except for the nightly session at the House of the Deer, life became very lonely. The rear compound of my house, however, backed on to a similar plot of ground in which stood a small wooden Burmese house occupied by a Burmese woman and a little Burmese girl. I never spoke to them, but we soon got to know each other by sight as I either ascended or descended the stairway at the back. Soon we were waving our greetings to each other, and sometimes I would throw a coin or some sweets over the fence for the child. They were friendly folk, and although I never spoke to them, these daily greetings brought a gleam of sunshine into an otherwise hopeless and terrible existence. Funds were running low, creditors were clamouring for the settlement of bills run up during time of plenty, and there was still no news from the north. Meanwhile my appetite for opium seemed insatiable. Even among the old Chinese *habitués* of the dens it had become a byword, and every rupee that I could scrape together had perforce to go to its satisfaction. What would happen when there was no longer any money wherewith to replenish the little wooden goblets? Then, indeed, having drained the cup of life to the dregs, would come the time for me to turn it over and say, as I had once said to an old Chinese magistrate on the Northeast Frontier, 'It is finished.'

Chapter XXV

THE BEGINNING OF THE END

It was New Year's Eve, and shortly before midnight I was making my way home from the House of the Deer. My circumstances were in a bad way, and I was finding it increasingly difficult to carry on. Rumours as to my position had, I knew, been circulating throughout the dens of Mandalay, passed on in whispers along the low platforms. They, who knew, were awaiting the crisis, and meanwhile the more cautious were beginning to withdraw themselves from my orbit, fearing lest they should be involved in any awkward situation. I found the knowledge of this very bitter and the more so on this night, the eve of a New Year, when, whatever the outlook, one may find in the company of friends expectations of better days to come. But I was to see this New Year in alone, and I found the prospect very depressing.

As I passed down a side lane near my house I came on a small knot of people standing round something white lying by the side of the road. Moved by curiosity, I joined the group and inquired what was the matter. Very excitedly they began to explain. A young Burman had been struck down only a few minutes previously, and the assailant had escaped in the darkness. I lifted the corner of the sheet and looked at the body. He had been a good-looking young man, in his early twenties and well-dressed. The murderer had done his job well. The weapon he had used, a *dah*, had bitten deeply into his victim's shoulder and nearly severed the head. The ground was stained with blood, but there was no sign of the weapon. I replaced the sheet, and, rounding the corner of the lane, entered my house. For a moment or two I stood in the back compound, considering whether I too would not be better dead.

I returned to the house, where in the lower rooms the servants were excitedly discussing the recent murder. Here I found that which I sought, a long, strong strap used for the fastening of one of my boxes. In the cool darkness of the compound I looped the strap through a grating over the door of one of the outhouses. The strap was strong, and the height was sufficient. The ethics of my intended act did not trouble me. Assuredly, I thought, it would entail a loss of merit; it was undoubtedly an act of retrogression. But, enslaved as I was, how much more might not be the merit which I might lose were I to continue in this hopeless struggle. Materially there was no one dependent upon me. Spiritually there was no one whom this act of self-destruction could touch, except myself, and I was prepared to risk the consequences.

The whole matter was very clear to me, but in the end it was not a question of ethics which turned the scale; it was something more human, more personal. First, as I gazed up at the strap hanging so invitingly from the grill, I thought of my unknown friends in the little bamboo hut which overlooked the compound. I thought of the kindly Burmese woman and her little girl and of the shock they might receive as they ascended their little staircase of the next morning and beheld the body of the unknown *thakin* swinging in the morning breeze. The second thought was one which might at first glance appear to be a strange one for an intending suicide to harbour. It was the picture which my body would present to those who discovered me—the protruding eyes, the swollen and blackened tongue. Thus even in the hour of death are we swayed by vanity!

Removing the strap, I passed up the outside staircase to my own apartments. It was midnight, and I felt very lonely. Something had to be done. It was too late to return to the House of the Deer, so I got out my little smoking-cabinet and sought tranquillity of spirit in the pipe. The little cabinet was the ingenious contrivance of a friend of mine, an old Chinese carpenter and a fellow-addict. The top and one side were hinged so that they could be opened out to form the tray on which the lamp and other accessories were placed. Inside the cabinet were partitions and racks for the lamp, needle, scraper, trimming-scissors, opium, and pipe, the last being a short one of ivory with a detachable jade mouthpiece. The box was lacquered in black and red, and was very neat.

I had not been smoking long when my eye was caught by a slight movement of the red velvet curtains which screened off the smoking platform. They parted, and in the opening appeared the figure of a Burman, dishevelled in appearance and furtive in manner. He had no head-dress, and I noted that his head was shaven. This meant that he was either a recently released monk or a recently liberated criminal. This matter of the shaven head often explained the custom of released prisoners hiding temporarily their marks of identification in the Noble Order of the Yellow Robe. But it was not these outward signs that particularly attracted my attention; it was the look in the man's eyes. They looked over me and past me in a stare that superficially represented that of an opium-smoker. I knew that it was not opium that had brought that background of horror into his unseeing gaze. He looked as a man might look who sees before him a vision of retribution, of the hell through which he must surely pass for some heinous sin very recently committed. Therefore it did not surprise me when I heard a soft patter of footsteps on the stairs, the faint creaking as a little shutter was raised above my ear, and the soft, sibilant whisper of my servants, 'Take care, *thakin*! This is the man.'

It was not surprising that he had come to me. Was it not known throughout the quarter—indeed, throughout the city—that I had once been U Nipana, the Gentle Monk? Many had been the transgressors who had found their way to my little smoking-room—thieves, adulterers, and now a murderer. But I too had transgressed no less than they, and the humility born of my bitter struggles I knew that never again would it be my lot or desire to judge.

I motioned him to the other side of the tray with a wave of my ivory pipe. We smoked turn and turn about, and as the minutes passed the look of horror passed from his eyes, and in its place came that expression of abstracted contemplation so familiar to the slaves of the White Poppy. Hour after hour we smoked, but never a word passed our lips. The first faint rays of light from the dawn of the New Year were filtering through the shutters when I laid down the pipe, and, my head still reclining on the hard little pillow, I fell asleep. When I awoke my midnight visitor had gone. But surely during those brief hours of trust between midnight and dawn he had acquired merit and the gratitude of a fellow-sufferer on the Wheel.

The New Year 1925 came in with little hope of relief or release. Weeks dragged by, and still there was no news from the north. Financially things were in a sorry plight. Money had to be found for opium, and gradually piece by piece my furniture and other salable objects began to disappear. Appeals to relations and friends, at first so fruitful, had now ceased to bear fruit. In the light of after-events I cannot blame them—it would have been throwing money down a bottomless pit. Meanwhile my creditors grew more insistent, and even the vaunted panacea of the opium failed to bring me relief from my anxieties. The 'Unborn To-morrow' was ever uppermost in my mind. It is in such things as these that the European-bred mind fails to identify itself with that of the Orient.

In vain I sought oblivion among the many drugs which were available to me. One long, long night I spent in the back room of the shop of an Indian who sold native remedies for every complaint from rheumatism to impotency. In the corner of the apartment squatted a young Pathan lad, a rose in his hair, playing *Zakhmy Dul* and other tunes of the North-west Frontier on a stringed instrument. My host and I, surrounded by the labelled bottles of his trade, dipped alternately from a brown three-cornered bottle of cocaine and a leaf on which was smeared the *chunna*, or burning lime. That night we consumed enough to kill three ordinary men, and when at length I made my way homeward it was as if I were walking on air, with a band of white heat behind my eyes. But it did not kill me; my struggle was not to end as easily as that.

Meanwhile my weight, in proportion to my height, had been reduced to the minimum. I ate practically nothing; the opium was all-sufficing. Twelve hours a day, sixteen hours a day, I smoked, and though temporary relief might be gained, I knew that the end was near.

It was in March that I decided to make a last bid for freedom. No news had come from the north, and I was in desperate straits. My plan was to go to Rangoon, and there, with the aid of a relation of the Poet's, to obtain employment which would keep me out in the open air and away from the temptation of the dens.

At the time I took this decision things were very bad. All my furniture, with the exception of my smoking apartment, had gone. The bed on which I slept and the chair on which I sat were already sold and were waiting but for my departure to be removed. My fare from Mandalay to Rangoon had been borrowed, with an additional five rupees in cash, from a High Court Judge with whom I had travelled to England in the previous year.

On the night of the 17th of March I bade farewell to Ba Ohn and The House of the Deer. I felt that they were in their way genuinely sorry, but I knew from my own experience that there was no life or warmth in their emotion. It was purely abstract.

Maung Ba Ohn, as delicately colourful as ever, made his farewell with that flickering, mocking smile playing about his red lips. It were as if he said, 'I have heard this before, *thakin*. No doubt we shall meet again.'

Ah Hpan was as uncouth but as genuine as he had always been. He had never tried to disguise his dislike of foreign devils, but he could not entirely forget a little service which I had once rendered him. His wife was less demonstrative but more convincing. There was a look in her eyes as I kissed her on the forehead which would have roused the young Zerbadi, Bah Maung, to an ecstasy of anticipatory delight.

As I passed down the line of smoking couples for the last time I could not help but feel a pang of regret that I could not wholly adjust myself to their way of life. It was the cursed handicap of one's upbringing, the standards which willy-nilly are implanted in us with our mother's milk. All along, ever since I had felt the desire to get behind this mask of the Orient, to submerge myself in it, I had felt this handicap. More than ever was it evident in my search after religion. The Christian faith had failed to satisfy me. I was of an extreme, if rather spasmodic, jealous temperament. If I thought that I loved (and I know now that I have never loved), I would have loved with such passion as to hate the thought of my beloved kneeling before a Creator in any way personal. It was this thought, together with the absurdity of any mortal having the faintest idea of the Infinite, which had led me to seek the Middle Way. Here was nothing personal, nothing defined.

I returned early to my house, feeling a little forlorn at parting from such old friends. But I had a lot to do in preparation for my departure on the morrow. On climbing the staircase to the upper floor I found little Ba Set and his mother awaiting me. They were very agitated. They had heard that I was going away. They had heard, but they were too courteous to reveal, that I was 'up against it.' Poor as they were, they had come to offer me a home as long as I cared to stay. I could have wept!

The mother left, but Ba Set stayed, curling his little body up in my big wicker armchair. From there he watched me as I packed my trunk, filled in my diary, and later settled down to a last pipe. As I smoked on, I forgot the little boy keeping vigil in the chair by the platform. My mind was full of the morrow and the possibilities of escape. Towards dawn, however, I put away my pipe and extinguished the little lamp. It was then that I became aware of the little curled figure asleep in the chair. He had been crying, and the tears had marked out grubby lines down his pale cheeks. He had been crying because of me, and, crying, had fallen asleep. I have said that I have never loved, but in that I was wrong because here, in this little Gethsemane, I felt within me the love that passeth the love of women.

Chapter XXVI

'IT IS FINISHED'

The morning of the 18th of March, 1925, broke hot and dry over Mandalay with the threat of a more intense heat to follow as the day advanced. Ba Set, a forlorn little figure, had trotted off home to his breakfast, promising to return at noon. The train was not due to leave until the evening, and everything was ready.

After a simple breakfast of tea and toast I lay down, still clad only in my sleeping-suit and dressing-gown, to smoke. It was about nine o'clock, and from where I lay I could see the denuded room and the packed trunks ready for transport. The usually rather exotic smoking-apartment was but a shell of its former self. Gone were the long red velvet curtains, the Persian carpets, the Japanese scroll-pictures. One by one they had gone to fill the little brown horn cylinder which contained my opium. It was a desolate scene, and the only gleam of comfort came from the little lamp over which I was moulding and fashioning the opium pellets. This lacquered cabinet, a real work of art, would be the last thing to be packed and, doubtless, the first thing to be disinterred on my arrival at Rangoon.

About eleven o'clock I brought the morning session to a close, but did not immediately pack the cabinet as it would be required in the afternoon. I was making some final entries in my diary, before putting it into the open trunk, when I heard a knocking on the outer door. Thinking that my boys would attend to it, I took no notice, but a few minutes later the knocking was repeated, and this time more peremptorily. Cursing the boys under my breath, I went down as I was, still in my dressing-gown, and opened the door. There, to my astonishment, I found a Burmese inspector of police and two constables. Behind them, looking rather white and uncomfortable, was an Englishman, the manager of a well-known firm of motor-dealers and a personal friend of mine. I invited them in and inquired their business. The inspector, with an importance suited to the occasion, informed me that he had a warrant for my arrest on a charge of attempting to abscond. The warrant, signed by a Burmese magistrate, had been issued at the request of my quondam friend, with whose firm I had had dealings running into many thousands of rupees during the previous two years. I expostulated, but in vain. Surely, I said, it is only a summons. But no—I had an outstanding liability with the firm, and this action had been taken as it had come to their ears that I was leaving that evening for Rangoon. I was thunderstruck; any idea of evading my liabilities had never entered my mind. Meanwhile the Englishman stood in the background, looking very ill at ease.

My mind worked rapidly, seeking a way of escape. I just have time to think, I said to myself—five minutes, ten minutes, a quarter of an hour if possible. I explained my position and that I had no thought of absconding. I requested that a letter might be conveyed from me to the High Court Judge who had made himself responsible for my fare to Rangoon. His name was a household word throughout Burma and had its desired effect. Hastily I wrote a note to him explaining what had happened. This note I gave to the Englishman, who agreed to deliver it to the Judge and bring back an answer within the half-hour. I now knew the reason why my boys had not been there to answer the door. The ship was sinking; the rats knew it and had left.

Telling the inspector that I must go upstairs to get dressed, I left them and ascended the outside staircase. The letter which I had sent meant nothing to me; it had been merely a subterfuge to gain time. I must think and think quickly. As I reached the top of the stairway I heard a ripple of laughter from the little hut at the rear of the compound. I turned and saw the Burmese woman and her child waving a morning greeting. I waved back and flung one of my five silver rupees over the fence for the little girl. Then I entered my room, locking and bolting the door behind me.

My mind was in a whirl, but of one, thing I was certain: I was not going to prison. Too many times during the past had I heard the howls of imprisoned men deprived of their opium. I had had some slight taste of it myself. No, there was only one way of escape.

I went to my trunk, and from it I took out a Browning automatic. Never had its steel-blue barrel looked more deadly. I placed it on a little table by the side of the large wicker armchair in which my Ba Set had cried himself to sleep the night before. On the table, by the side of the automatic, I placed the little brass representation of the Buddha which had been my constant companion for ten years. For a minute or two I considered the horn opium container. It was nearly full, ready stocked for my trip to Rangoon. I felt that it might ease my passage were I to swallow the contents, but some vague recollections of 'elementals,' which hindered the separation of the soul from the body after death, dissuaded me.

My memories of these moments are still very clear. I found myself repeating some lines of Kipling's:

> *Just roll to yer rifle and blow out yer brains,*
> *And go to yer Gawd like a soldier.*

Yes, that was how it must be done. Seating myself in the armchair, I took up the automatic and pulled back the breech-block, thus letting the first cartridge slip into place. It was a terrible sound and a terrible moment. There are people who say, glibly enough, that to commit suicide is a cowardly act. They don't know what they are talking about. It is on occasions such as these that a man, of his own free will, comes face to face with his Maker... and calls His bluff.

I was afraid, horribly afraid, and the palms of my hands were sweaty as on that day, many years before, when I, then a school-boy, had lifted my eyes to the Host in spite of the warning of the old French *bonne* that it would make me blind.

But even in that hour of death—so vain are the thoughts of man—the mode of my dispatch presented a problem of meticulous nicety. Since I was a very third-rate shot, my first impulse was to bite on the barrel, but a few seconds' reflection was sufficient to change my mid. That would, I thought, result in an unsightly corpse, with the back of the head blown out. The correct way, according to the tenets of common usage, was to fire through the temple. It is strange, is it not, that men should be swayed thus in their final hour?

Accordingly I rested my arm on the side of the chair and raised the automatic to my right temple. The little figure of the Buddha, the All-wise, the All-compassionate, gazed down upon me with his inscrutable eyes, and, fixing my gaze on him, I pulled the trigger. There was a terrific explosion, and then...

I felt myself falling, falling, falling through interminable space. Down and down I fell, and as I fell I thought of the reference in the Creed to 'He descended into hell.' At length the descent ceased, and before me I saw a Veil, a Veil of Red, behind which I could hear voices speaking. Once again my innate curiosity was roused, and I wondered whom I should see when the Veil was rent. But it was not to be rent for me. I found myself being whirled round and round as though attached to the rim of some gigantic wheel. Then I began to ascend through the vastness of space. As I rose I again bethought me of the Creed, 'He ascended into heaven,' and I felt more cheerful. The upward sweep ceased and then...

Gradually feeling came back to my hands, and I felt beneath them the corrugations of the arms of the wicker chair. My God, I thought, I have failed again. A failure all my life, I couldn't even make a decent job of ending it. But there was still the red mist before my eyes, and I guessed that it must be blood. I put up my hand to wipe it away, and then, for the first time in my life, I screamed. My eyeballs had been blown out and were hanging down on my cheeks. At the same time I became aware of a violent banging at the locked and bolted door. The police below, who had heard the shot, were trying to break in. My mind once again became crystal-clear. The automatic had fallen from my hand, but I remembered that there were still in it five unexpended rounds. I would make no mistake about it this time. I would bite on the barrel.

But, even as these thoughts passed through my mind, I knew that I must be wary. I was blind, and it would not do to lose myself in the search for the lost automatic. So I hooked my right ankle round the front right leg of the chair and, going down on my hands and knees, I felt round for the Browning. But I could not find it, and it was thus, bloody and groping, that, breaking open the door, they found me.

They led me, very tenderly, down the stairs, through the lower rooms and out into the warmth of the noontide sun. As I stumbled down the steps to the street a car drew up, stopped an instant, and drove off at a breakneck speed. It was, as I guessed, the Englishman.

As he had not even stopped to drive me in his car to the hospital, my escort called a *tikka gharri*. Making my way towards this with the help of the kindly policemen, I suddenly felt my knees clasped about by a pair of small arms while convulsive sobs came from a little figure, apparently kneeling in the dust. It was Ba Set. Very gently and very carefully, for every movement was an agony to me, I put down my hand and disengaged the little arms from about my legs. For an instant my hand rested on the faithful head of this Burmese boy, and then I entered the waiting *gharri* and was driven off to the hospital.

That drive through the midday heat of Mandalay was torture unbearable; the jolting, the heat, and the flies playing havoc with my exposed and pendent eyeballs. After what seemed an interminable time we reached the hospital, and I was led in to the office. From out of the darkness I heard the voice, the typical voice, of a baboo asking me my name and address. Even in such extremities the proprieties must be observed. Then he asked me my religion.

It must be remembered that I thought that I was going to die, that I was dying, and under such circumstances this is a question which cannot be treated lightly. Conversion was not a matter to be treated with an easy going acceptance. Much as I admired the work of Christian missionaries, especially those of the Salvation Army and the Roman Catholic Church, among the lepers and the fallen in the East, I still maintained that the principle of conversion was erroneous. The Eurasian, so susceptible to the incense and ceremonial of the Roman Church, can, in private life, be outside the pale and influenced by any superstition inherited from his Asiatic forbears. In the same way, I was to learn later that the West African negro, nominally a Roman Catholic, would in the hour of trouble turn to the heathenish arts of the witch-doctor, his hereditary priest. And so it is the same with all of us. However much our reason may tend to guide us towards a certain line of thought, in the hour of danger, in the hour of death, we return to that religion which we imbibed with our mother's milk. Thus are we biassed and prejudiced in our search for wisdom. If I had my way I would teach to the young only those ethics which are common to all religions. These are the laws which have evolved naturally throughout the ages and which are common to all great religions: the desire for truth, the abhorrence of murder and adultery, and the blessing of universal love. Then, when such men and maidens should have attained the years of discretion, I should open to them the teachings of such great men as the Buddha, the Christ, and Mohammed. They would then be free to choose the way, not that it mattered much which way they chose as, in my belief, they all lead to the same goal.

But when this baboo put this same question to me I had no time in which to reason such matters out. I was dying, and at that time it seemed to me a matter of extreme importance. But I considered these kindly Burmese folk whom I had known and loved so well and who were even then waiting on my answer, and I thank God that I had the decency to reply, 'Buddhist.'

After my examination an English Sister took me in hand. I was laid on a couch, where she bared my arm preparatory to the insertion of the blessed needle. As she gathered up the skin I heard her exclaim, 'Whatever are these red marks?'

Through my pain the recollection came back to me of the old hermit in the little hut without the gates of the monastery. I laughed a little weakly. 'Oh! that!' I said. 'That is only a charm.' 'Queer,' I thought to myself as the needle slid into my flesh, 'queer that I should have forgotten about that. A charm against death from a bullet wound! But there was something else.' And as I sank back into the depths of merciful oblivion I seemed to hear again the voice of the old Chinese monk warning me that if I disregarded his advice I should have to suffer in darkness.

Chapter XXVII

BURMA ROAD

It is a year later, and I am sitting in an upper room in a suburban house on the outskirts of London. The only reminders of the past which I know to be present are a little worn figure of the Buddha on the table by my side, a framed inscription on the wall which tells curious visitors that 'The banana is great, but the skin is greater,' and... my memories.

As I sat musing there I thought of the happenings which had led to my miraculous deliverance; for miraculous it certainly had been. Addiction to drugs, and in particular drugs derived from opium, is not a habit lightly to be cast aside. You may attempt to escape by substituting one drug for another, as I had intended substituting morphia for opium-smoking; you may enter special nursing-homes or endeavour to conquer the habit through the science of religion. But, from my own experience of opium-smoking, all these avenues of escape, however much they may be advocated by their special devotees, are useless. Unless you are a man of exceptional will-power, you will be drawn back as irresistibly as an iron filing to a magnet. And you must remember that when you have been smoking opium for two years your will-power is at a minimum. The only thing that will cure you is a shock, a sudden and a devastating shock, which may be a hard price to pay, but, believe me, it is worth it. I had the good fortune to receive such a shock. I had recovered consciousness to find myself lying in bed, my head well and truly bandaged. I could see nothing, but as time passed I began to experience the old uneasiness which told me that it must be nearing six o'clock in the evening. In answer to my call, the sister came to me and gave me some opium pills. This, I thought, is how things should have been managed on board that boat. My uneasiness was temporarily abated, and, in spite of the pain, I slept. The next day the surgeon had come and removed my bandages. He asked me if I could see anything. I replied that I believed that I could see if I could open my eyes. I did not realize at the time that they were already wide open and inflamed. I suppose that this convinced him of the uselessness of trying to save my sight, because the next day he told me that the eyes would have to be removed.

I did not mind. Nothing seemed to matter to me then. The opium pills relieved my uneasiness, and, except for cramps in my stomach as the nurses began to feed me up, I seemed to exist in a state of living death. But although my head, with the exception of the immediate vicinity of my eyes, was as dead as a board, my mind was very alert. The bullet had entered at the right temple and passed behind the nose on its way out of my left eye. The surgeon said that it was by a miracle, a fraction of an inch, that I had escaped death. But such miracles did not interest me; I wanted to die. I hoped that when I went under the anæsthetic it would be the end. But it was not to be so easy; I still had to live and learn. And meanwhile the uneasiness in my body grew less and less as the opium pills were daily decreased. I still thought of the little lamps being lit in the dens down in the neighbourhood of the House of the Deer, but I realized the futility of trying to reach them, especially as now I was aware that there was a police guard outside the doors of my room. The Padre, the same padre who had been with me on the evening when the Poet and I had first gone down to the Chinese eating-house, came to visit me. He talked a lot to me about God and... almost he persuaded me to be a Christian. But I knew the Padre, and I had known U Nyana, of the Ma-soe-yin-kyaung-daik, and it was the latter's tolerance which finally triumphed over the bigotry of the Christian faith. U Nyana had been so understanding, so compassionate; he had not insisted on his way, the Middle Way, being the only way. I did not want a Dictator for my God. I did not even want my God to be a personal God. In my opinion, the Buddha had been a man who, by dint of self-renunciation and deep meditation, had attained perfection and at the end had been absorbed into the Spirit of Goodness and thus become one with God. This was the Divine Fusion to which all could attain.

As the days passed by and the dry heat of Mandalay burned like fire through my body the ease from the terror increased, and my mind reverted to Ba Set and to how he was faring. No news could I obtain. Now and again a friend would take me for a drive through the outskirts of the city, but never would they allow me to be within earshot of the native quarter.

A month elapsed, and then I was moved to Rangoon. I went to the home of my friend, the Poet, and there amidst congenial surroundings and loving care I found a certain measure of peace. Any acute craving for opium had passed; I found too much to do in carrying out the normal routine of life. But I knew that as long as I remained in Burma the call of the little lamps would be there.

It was difficult to obtain a passage back to England. Three ships ejected me as soon as they learned that I was an attempted suicide. Sailors are superstitious, and I cannot blame them. At length a ship turned up whose medical officer, a young Scotsman, was prepared to

5. *The Author Today* [1942].

take the risk. He took me into his own cabin and tended me throughout the voyage in the manner which one might expect from a member of that honourable profession. How different he was from that supercilious medico of my former voyage. With his aid, and that of the trained nurse who accompanied me, I regained sanity of mind, and by the time I reached England was prepared to face my new life.

Meanwhile I considered my future and the next stretch of the road which I was to tread. I realized that for a space I should have to suffer myself to be led. But I also knew that that would not always be the case; the time would come when I should step out once again, maybe a little falteringly, but... alone. I had to prepare and train myself to that end.

Since my return I had received a letter from that Buddhist Association to which I had been affiliated thanking me for my declaration of faith at the time of my trial and telling me that every day during my stay at Mandalay little Ba Set had waited outside the hospital with newly gathered flowers for me, but had been denied admittance. I never knew of this, and can you blame me if it hardened my heart against the Christian belief? Little Ba Set, the ever-faithful, surely he must have attained to great merit. With eyes up-lifted, he never noticed the feet of clay.

And thus I mused in my room in that little suburban villa. I had gone through hell, but I had come safely into harbour. I did not regret any of it, and all through the future there would be the memory little Ba Set and his flowers—that was reward enough.

A knock broke in on my meditations. There entered a friend who had a letter containing a copy of my birth certificate. This was necessary, as I had decided to enter the Massage School of the National Institute for the Blind. Out of curiosity I asked her for the details of the certificate. I knew that I had been born in Stoke Newington, but apart from that I had no particulars, as my parents had moved shortly after my birth. 'Burma Road', she said. My heart seemed to miss a beat at the words. Was this, then, the explanation of it all? Had my destiny been fulfilled and the Wheel turned full circle?

www.ingramcontent.com/pod-product-compliance
Lightning Source LLC
Chambersburg PA
CBHW022132160426
43197CB00009B/1255